Do It All with Word®

Self-Publication (and More!) Using Only Word®

By Evelyn Sabbag

ISBN: 0983550670
ISBN-13: 978-0-9835506-7-9

DEDICATION

To all the writers who struggle with applications meant to make our lives easier.

And to my beloved husband, Doug, who not only tolerates, but encourages, my unending projects.

Evelyn Sabbag

Table of Contents

List of Figures

Chapter 1.**Self-Publication**

1.1.   Introduction

Self-publication is gaining ground as a respected venue for authors; more and more are becoming quite successful and earning a comfortable living. Unfortunately, publishing your own book means that you're not just a writer anymore. You're the copy editor, the print setter, the graphic artist, the proofreader, the logistician, the distributor, publicist and marketer. In short, you've become a publisher. And there's a plethora of information about how to do this. The resources consist of simple Do-It-Yourself (DIY) instructions to services willing to churn out the hands on work for you. The expenditures can range from a few dollars for the self-help books to several thousand for a turnkey solution. This book is a DIY solution that will enable you to publish your first book.

But why is this guide different from the scores of others out there? First, the only application you have to purchase is Microsoft Word®. This program can accomplish everything from the interior formatting to the cover layout. There's no need to buy expensive publishing or image manipulation software. Second, my credentials include not just self-publishing, but decades of computer technology experience. When I published my first book, the rework was tedious and exhausting because I didn't know when each step in the process had to occur. As a computer professional and executive trainer, I'm supplying a roadmap that will minimize the do-overs.

Keep in mind that this guide is strictly to inform on the technical aspects of self-publishing; it doesn't guarantee that you'll retire on the proceeds of your novels. It's not that it can't happen—there are many self-published authors living comfortably on what they've accomplished. However, the marketing portion of self-publication is beyond the scope of this book. Once I figure out that process, I'll publish the results. In the meantime, check out my musings on my blog, Twitter and FaceBook

The organization of this book is such that each chapter and section is stand-alone and you can move back and forth to get the information you need. In fact, you'll find that you may *have* to move back and forth and that's okay. For example, to complete the book's interior, an ISBN (International Standard Book Number) is required. If you obtain an ISBN from an identifier service, you should submit the size and weight of the book. Which you won't know until you complete the interior of the book. Which requires an ISBN. Don't worry; all that will be covered in the appropriate section.

1.2.   Assessing the Book

Before sending your manuscript out into the world, ask the following questions.

1.   Is the manuscript complete?
2.   Has the text been carefully reviewed for typos, grammar and syntax?
3.   Has anyone other than you read the manuscript?

4. If the answer to all three questions is yes and you already have a completed, polished manuscript, move ahead to either **Chapter 2** for a Print on Demand (POD) paperback or **Chapter 6** for an eBook.

While it may seem obvious, completing the manuscript is the first step in self-publishing. And this requires hard work, time, sacrifice and money. Once the manuscript is complete, a professional copyediting is a good idea. This is one of three areas that I believe warrant financial outlay. Quality artwork is another, which will be covered in **Chapter 4 CS—Cover Art,** and ISBNs, section **2.5.2 ISBN**. Not only does a professional copyeditor correct typos and grammatical errors, it's someone who has a professional distance and will give an honest review. After the editing, having one or more readers give feedback can help immeasurably in identifying trouble spots. It takes a thick hide, but better earlier than later when the whole world can take pot shots at your hard work.

A few steps to keep in mind as you're building your manuscript.

1. Save often. Autosave will protect in the event of a computer lockup, but it will be only as good as the last autosave. And it can be confusing to know which file to restore. <**CTRL**><**S**> is quick and easy and saves a world of grief.

2. Using the automatic features such as captions, cross-references and table of contents can save time, but only if you use them properly. Periodically, enter <**CTRL**><**A**> (select all), followed by <**F9**> (update all). If a Table of Contents, Figures or Tables has been created, you will be given the option to <**Update page numbers only**> or <**Update entire table**>. It's a good idea to always update the entire table.

3. Once the entire document has been updated, review each page to ensure headings, captions, figures, etc. haven't inadvertently moved. And yes, they can move, seemingly on their own. It's because Word® has formatting marks that are hidden and next to impossible to remove. It's better to just look it over, make sure it appears visually appealing and move on. Creating a document in Word® is mostly about changing, checking, changing and checking…

4. These directions are based on Word 2010®. The first obstacle to using Word® is knowing that certain functions exist. The seconds is knowing what they're called. If you use a different version and something doesn't match, use the name of the feature / function and do an Internet search. In the words of the X-Files – *the answer's out there...*

And what would any book be without a disclaimer? Unfortunately, the information in this workbook is only guaranteed at the time of publication. Websites change; print doesn't. A cool feature on Amazon is that if you buy a print copy, you receive the eBook for free. I will update the eBook with changes if/when they occur and you should reference that medium to keep on top of this changing world. And please, if you find a section confusing or <**GASP**>, incorrect, please let me know. Or if you just need help. You can reach me at info@TriumphCharters.com, post questions on Amazon, and/or check out my website at http://www.triumphcharters.com/books.html. I also frequent Twitter, @ESabbagAuthor , and pontificate on my blog at http://evelynsabbag.blogspot.com/ . I'd love to hear from you!

Chapter 2. CreateSpace(CS)—New Project

2.1. Introduction

CreateSpace (CS) is Amazon's Print on Demand (POD) publisher. There are no minimum quantity buys, the customer support is responsive and friendly, the results are high quality and you're able to tap into Amazon's worldwide distribution. If you don't have a CS account and aren't sure how to proceed, **Chapter 8 Setting up a CreateSpace Account** gives guidance on this topic.

2.2. Log In to Existing Account

Access your account by navigating to www.CreateSpace.com. Fill in the email account and password (**Figure 1 - 1**), and click on **<Log In>** as indicated in **Figure 1- 2**.

Figure 1. CS Website—Log In to Existing Account

2.3. PC Folder Structure

Create the following project folders on your laptop. Bold type indicates actual name. Replace *Name of Book* with the actual name of your book

1. Top Folder: *Name of Book*
    a. Secondary Folder 1: **Cover Art**—*Name of Book*
    b. Secondary Folder 2: **eBook**—*Name of Book*
    c. Secondary Folder 3: **Images**—*Name of Book*
    d. Secondary Folder 4: **Paperback**—*Name of Book*
    e. Secondary Folder 5: **Templates**—*Name of Book*

When finished, the folder structure should resemble that in **Figure 2.**

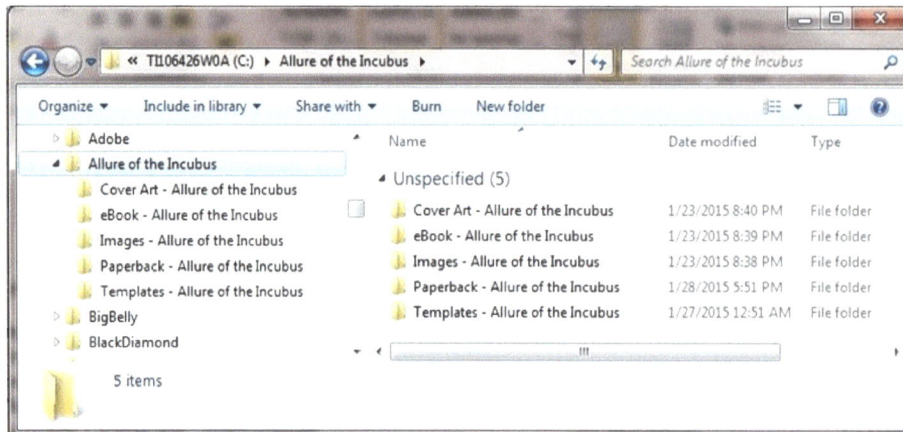

Figure 2. PC Folder Structure

2.4. Add New Title

After logging into your CreateSpace account, the Member Dashboard in **Figure 3** should appear. Click on **<Add New Title>, Figure 3-1**.

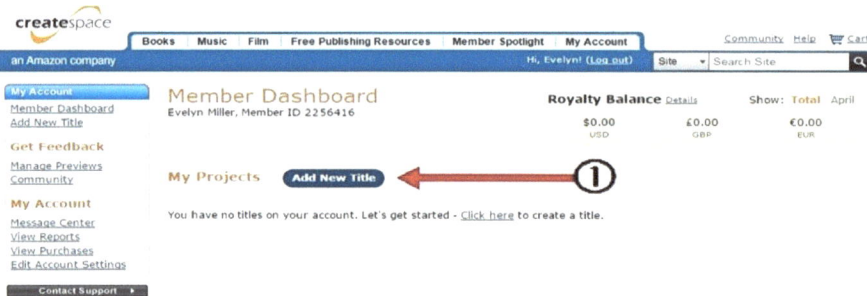

Figure 3. CS—Member Dashboard: Add New Title

2.5. New Project Title

Once you click on **<Add New Title>**, the screen in **Figure 4** should appear. Type the name of your book in the field under **<Tell us the name of your project>** (**Figure 4-1**) and click **<Paperback>** (**Figure 4-2**). Once you're satisfied with the title, select **<Expert/Get Started>** (**Figure 4-3**).

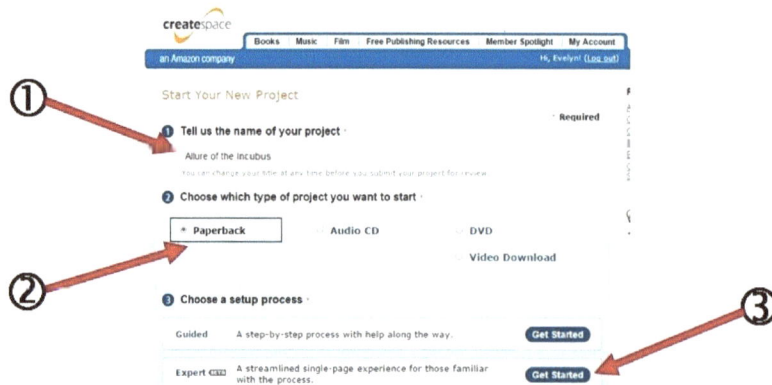

Figure 4. CS—Start Your New Project

Note: The name of your project does not have to match your book title, but make it something meaningful, not "Project 1" or "My New Project."

Note: The book title can change right up until publication.

Note: Once you click <**Get Started**>, you can select the project from the Member Dashboard the next time you log in (**Figure 5-1**).

Figure 5. CS—Member Dashboard with Project

2.6. Project Homepage

After clicking on the project (**Figure 5**), the Project Homepage (**Figure 6**) will appear. The **Setup** discussed in the following sections will originate from this page.

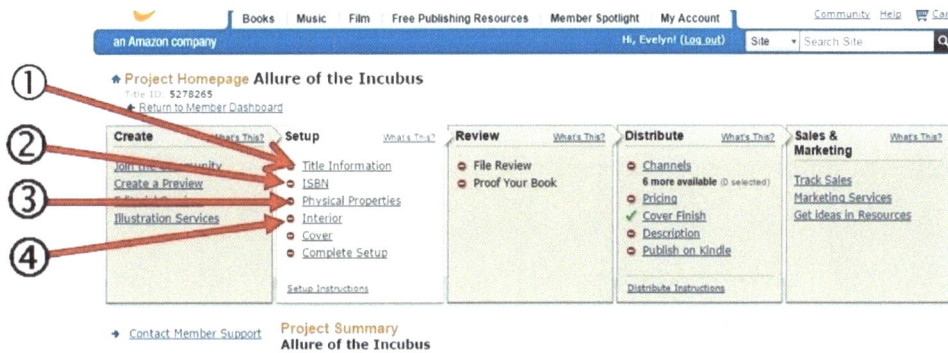

Figure 6. CS—Project Homepage

2.6.1. Title Information

Click on <**Title Information**> (**Figure 6-1**). The next steps are to fill in the information in **Figure 7**.

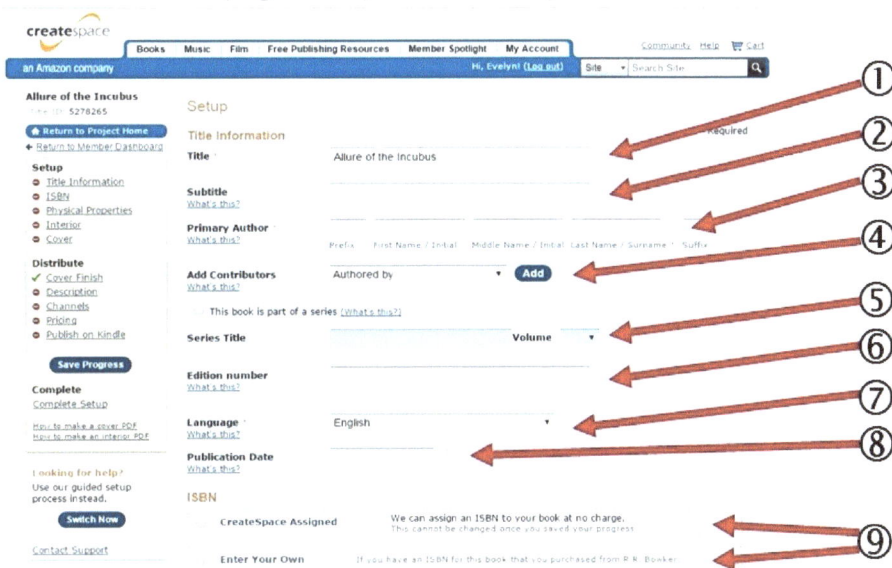

Figure 7. CS—Title Information - Filled in for *Allure of the Incubus*

Note: Any of the following information that is filled in must match the ISBN information exactly, regardless of whether it is required or optional.

Note: Fields marked with an '*****' are required.

1 *Title—Fill in the name of the book exactly as it will be displayed on the book jacket. It will be used for search engines and indexing.

2 *Subtitle* (Optional)—This verbiage is concatenated onto the title and will appear as *Title: Subtitle*. Note that the colon is added by the distributing entity.

3 *Primary Author—The name or pseudonym of the author exactly as it should be displayed in the distribution catalogue. This is used by search engines and to set up your author's page. If you use initials or a pseudonym, Amazon will not allow you to input your real name just because you say so.

4 *Add Contributors* (Optional)—Use the drop down menu (indicated by the arrow) to select a function, click <**Add**> and then add the associated name. Examples would be additional authors, editors, etc.

5 *This book is part of a series* (Optional)—Click this check box if the book is in a series. If it is, also fill in <**Series Title**> and the <**Volume #**>. Both of these fields are grayed out until the check box is clicked.

6 *Edition Number* (Optional)—Fill in if appropriate. Otherwise, leave it blank.

7 *Language—Defaults to English. Use the drop down menu to select the appropriate language.

8 *Publication Date* (Optional)—**DO NOT FILL THIS IN**. Once filled in, it cannot be modified. If left blank, CreateSpace will automatically update the field once the book is submitted for publication.

2.6.2. ISBN

Scroll down on the Title Information page(**Figure 7**) or select ISBN from the project homepage (**Figure 6-2**). There are two selections for the ISBN (**Figure 8**), **CreateSpace Assigned** and **Enter Your Own**.

Note: If a CreateSpace ISBN has been selected and the progress saved, this **CANNOT** be changed. For now, leave this selection blank. CreateSpace will squawk, but it won't stop you from moving forward.

Note: Every media format requires a unique ISBN. A paperback and an ebook with the same content require two separate ISBN's.

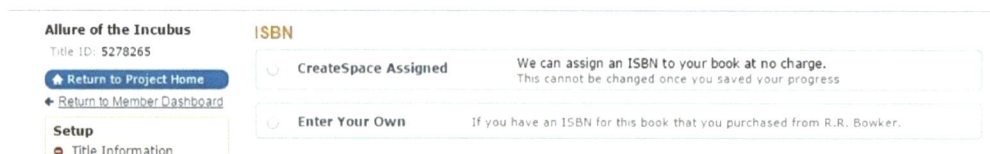

Figure 8. CS—ISBN Selection

2.6.2.1. CreateSpace Assigned

a. This selection is provided by CreateSpace for no cost (free).

b. All distribution channels through CreateSpace are available, including libraries and academic institutions.

c. The imprint will display *CreateSpace Independent Publishing Platform*.

d. **The book is only distributable** through the CreateSpace Independent Publishing Platform. It can be sold through Amazon, the CreateSpace eBookstore and all other associated channels, but cannot be sold through Barnes & Noble, or other retailers.

e. CreateSpace or Amazon DOES NOT own the content.

f. If the book is started with a free ISBN, a new Edition can be created with your own ISBN down the road. However, it must have significant changes such as title, content, trim size, etc.

g. Once progress is saved, this choice is **Locked** (**Figure 9**).

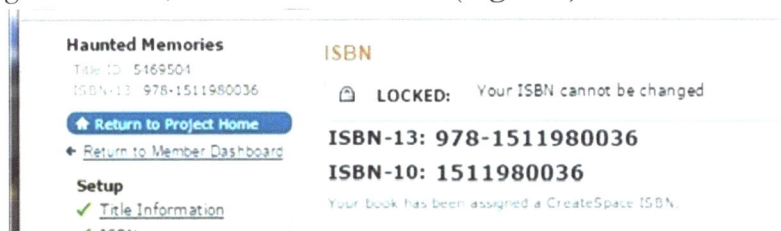

Figure 9. CS—CreateSpace Supplied ISBN

2.6.2.2. Enter Your Own

Note: This is my choice. My **imprint** (publisher / corporation name) is *Triumph Ventures, Inc.*

a. Bowker® Identification Services sells ISBN's that are completely owned and controlled by you (https://www.myidentifiers.com).

b. Discounts can be realized by purchasing ISBN's in quantity. 1 ISBN/$125, 10/$295, 100/$575.

c. Distribution is not limited to CreateSpace and its associated channels.

d. The book is not automatically available to libraries and academic institutions, but can be provided independently.

e. You provide the publisher's name (imprint). While not required, I strongly recommend incorporation to protect your rights and future income. Why not get the credit you deserve?

f. This choice can be modified any time up to submitting the files for review, even if progress is saved. CreateSpace <u>wants</u> you to use their imprint; thus, it's easier to switch to the dark side.

2.6.3. Physical Properties

The physical properties (**Figure 10**) include the interior type, the paper color and the trim size. This information can be selected from the Project Homepage (**Figure 6-3**) or scroll down from the Title Information (**Figure 7**).

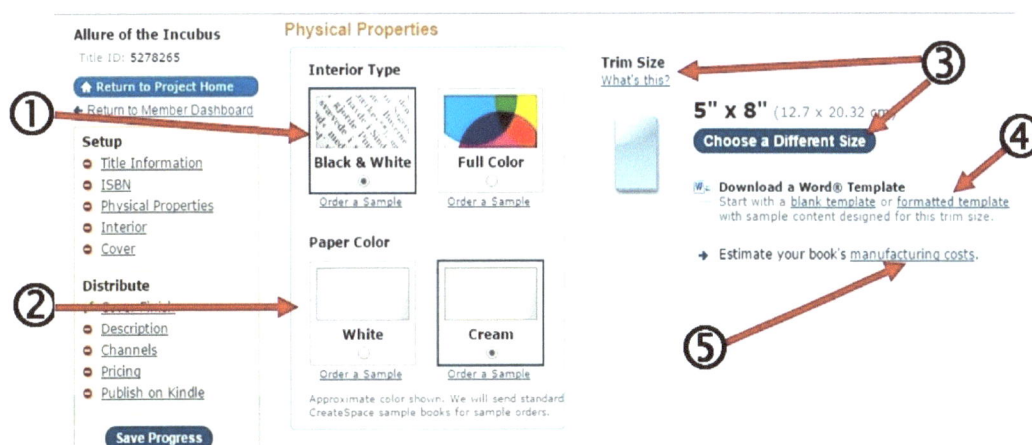

Figure 10. CS—Physical Properties

1. Interior Type

    Note: The interior type significantly affects the cost of printing. Color is approximately 3 times more expensive than black and white. How to estimate costs is discussed in a later section.

    a. **Black & White:** Typical for most novels, particularly with either no graphics or with only black and white line drawings or photographs.

   b. **Full Color:** Appropriate for graphic novels, children's picture books and books that contain a significant amount of figures.

2. Paper Color

   a. **White:** Required if *Full Color* interior is selected; good for How-To books where stark contrast is desired.

   b. **Cream:** easier than white on the eyes.

Note: If the correct trim size (*Industry Standard*) is not selected, the book will not be distributable through all channels.

- Industry standard trim sizes for **white paper** are: 5.5" x 8.5", 6" x 9", 6.14" x 9.21", 7" x 10", 8" x 10", 8.5" x 8.5" or 8.5" x 11". The book you're reading is 8.5" x 11".

- Industry standard trim sizes for **cream paper** are: 5"x8", 5.25"x8", 5.5"x8.5", or 6"x9".

3. Trim Size: To determine the correct size, look at books similar to your project. Note the number of pages, font size and overall dimensions. The default trim size on the project page is 6" x 9". Click on <**Choose a different size**> (**Figure 10-3**) if this is not the size appropriate for your project. Look at the drop down menu (**Figure 11**) and select a trim size closest to the books you like.

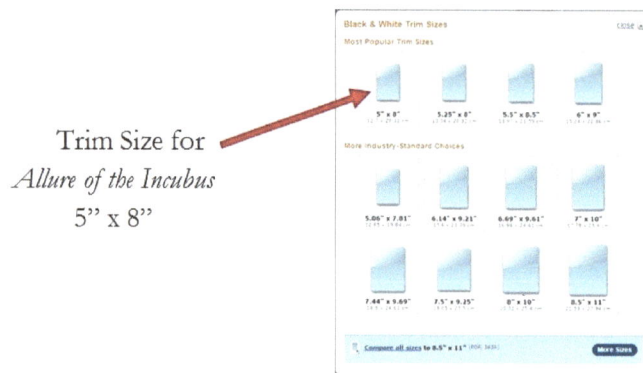

Trim Size for
Allure of the Incubus
5" x 8"

Figure 11. CS—Trim Sizes

There are many sizes to choose from, even custom. However, it's important to consider what your goals are. The trim size determines how many books fit into a standard shipping carton. If an industry standard is chosen, the book is accepted by more channels. Once you reach J. K. Rawlings or Stephen King status, you can dictate any size you want. For now, stick with the industry standards and come across as a partner more channels will want to work with.

2.6.4. Download a Word ® Template

Click on <**formatted template**> (**Figure 10-4**). The formatted template corresponding to the selected trim size will automatically download. Copy the file to the templates folder previously created for this project (**Section 2.3, 1.e. Secondary Folder 5: Templates—***Name of Book***). This will be used in **Chapter 3. CS—Interior Formatting.**

2.6.5. Estimating your book's manufacturing costs

Member Order Calculator: From the project page, scroll to the middle of the page and click on <**manufacturing costs**> (**Figure 10-5**). This will display the **Member Order Calculator**.

If not on the project page, scroll to the top of any page and click on the <**Books**> tab. On the drop down menu, select <**Publish a Trade Paperback**> (**Figure 12-1**).

Figure 12. CS—Estimating Your Book's Manufacturing Costs

On the resulting page, click on **<Buying Copies>** (**Figure 13-1**) and scroll down to the Member Order Calculator (**Figure 14**).

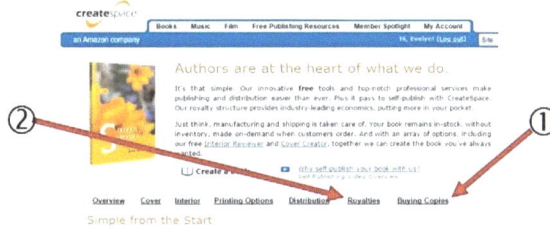

Figure 13. CS—Buying Copies

Figure 14. CS—Member Order Calculator

Fill in the values selected for this project and click <**Calculate**>. This is what the book will cost if ordered directly from your CreateSpace account, not including shipping costs.

Note: Color pages are more expensive than Black and White, but are not relative to the size of the pages, only to the quantity. That is, a book with a trim size of 6"x9" will cost the same as a trim size of 8.5"x11". Keep this in mind when setting up books with color graphics. Select the larger size, if it makes sense, as the cost will be the same and the pictures will be easier to view.

Royalties: One of the benefits of publishing a book through CreateSpace is that global distribution is included. To facilitate this feature, a portion of the book is retained by Amazon / CreateSpace. Setting the list price is dependent on what you as the publisher would like to see as your profit. Keep the price reasonable, but ensure you aren't paying any of the channels for the privilege of carrying your book.

Scroll to the top of the page and click on the tab entitled <**Royalties**> (**Figure 13-2**). Scroll down to the <**Royalty Calculator**> (**Figure 15**). Fill in the values selected for this project, determine a list price and click <**Calculate**>. Adjust the list price until there are no negative Royalty values.

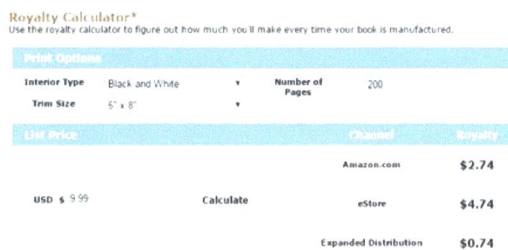

Figure 15. CS—Royalty Calculator

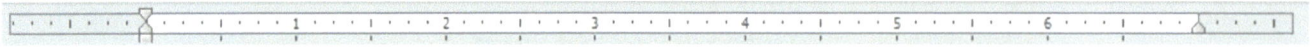

Chapter 3.**CS—Interior Formatting**

3.1. Introduction

CreateSpace takes a lot of the mystery out of creating a Print Ready manuscript by supplying templates, which are extremely useful. However, they also introduce a lot of mystery. If the author doesn't understand the underpinnings of Word®, making the pages look as envisioned can be a frustrating task. As a result, in this user's guide, the templates are used to set up the margins and some formatting, but the custom style pages (CSP) will only be emulated, and, ultimately, eliminated.

3.2. Preparing the Manuscript Template

Copy the formatted template from the **Templates** folder to the working **Paperback** folder and rename it to reflect the current project. Detailed steps are outlined below.

1. Navigate to the folder created in section **2.3 PC Folder Structure, 1.e, <Templates – *Name of Book*>**.
2. Right click on the downloaded template and select <**Copy**>.
3. Navigate to the folder **<Paperback-*Name of Book*>** (**2.3 PC Folder Structure, 1.d**).
4. Right click anywhere in the folder area and select **<Paste>**.
5. Right click on the file and select **<Rename>**.
6. Type in the title ***Name of Book*-5x8**.docx (or .doc as required by the installed version of Word®) where 5x8 is replaced by the trim size of your book. '.'s are okay, as in 5.5x8.5.

3.3. Section Content

The first step is to add in content for all sections except for the chapters. If a Table of Contents (TOC) is desired, leave the section intact, but don't fill in the information. The chapter headings will be set up to update the TOC automatically.

Open the renamed file with Word®. On the toolbar, click the **<Home>** tab. Ensure the <**Show/Hide Formatting Marks>** symbol (**Figure 16**) is highlighted. For the remainder of the formatting the parenthetical marks must be visible.

Note: My husband really hates this feature, but when setting up for print, this is invaluable. Trust me.

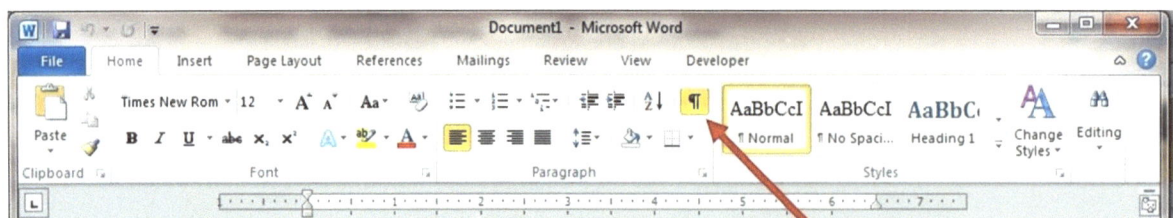

Figure 16. CS—Show / Hide Formatting Marks

At this point, fill in as many sections as you can. This includes **Dedication**, **Acknowledgements**, **About the Author**, and so on. If you have an ISBN, include this and the imprint (publisher's name) on the page just after the **Title** page. Don't be concerned if you're not prepared for all the sections. You can work back and forth between the areas as you go.

To keep the formatting intact, do not over write the paragraph marks. **Figure 17** shows the title page as an example. The new paragraph marks indicate hard returns / line feeds created by pressing <**Enter**> (**Figure 17-1**) to ensure the title is centered correctly. If necessary, delete or add paragraph marks.

Note: Make sure all section breaks (**Figure 17**-**2**) remain intact, unless an entire section is removed.

Note: A section break may create a new page, but is different from a page break. A section break can have special formatting associated only with that section. Page numbers are one example. This is why some sections have *i, ii, iii…* and others have 1, 2, 3…

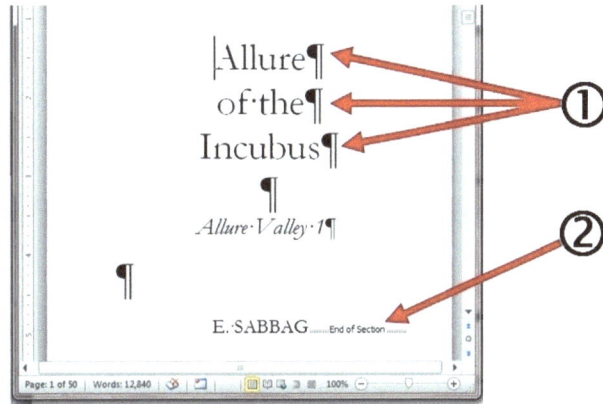

Figure 17. CS—Formatting Marks / Section Break

Note: Some sections such as the **Title**, **Dedication**, **Table of Contents**, and others may be centered, which could interfere with desired alignment. To modify the page alignment, select <**Page Layout**>, then the down arrow on the <**Page Setup**>, then the <**Layout**> tab as shown in **Figure 18-1**. Select the desired alignment using the drop down menu, *Top, Center, Justified* or *Bottom*.

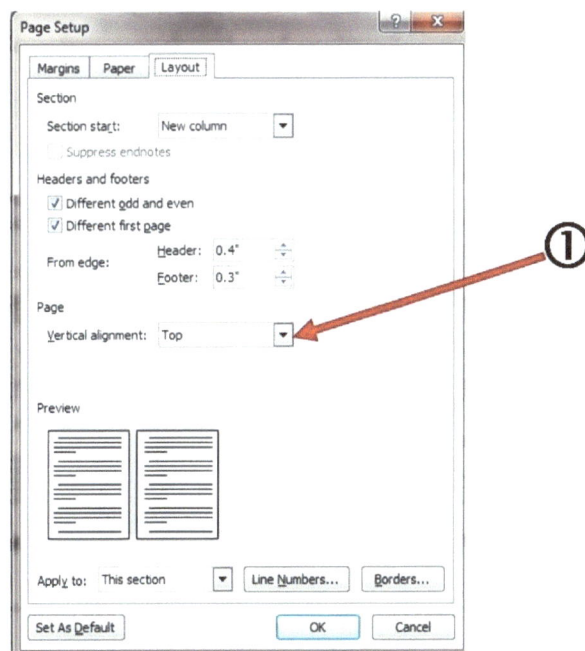

Figure 18. CS—Page Alignment

Highlight the text within the desired sections up to, but without overwriting the <**End of Section**> indicators (**Figure 19**). Type desired text (**Figure 19**). If you accidentally overwrite a section break (***End of Section***), use <**Undo**> and try again.

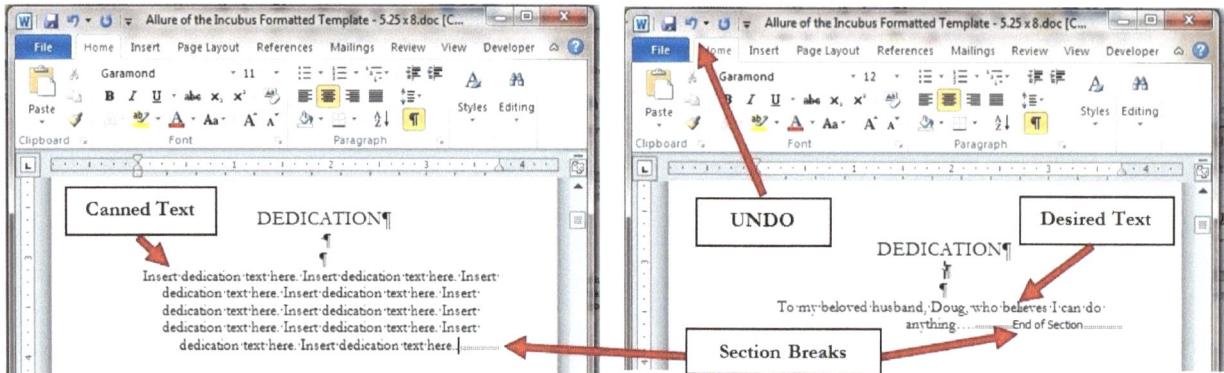

Figure 19. CS—Replacing Canned Text with Actual Content

Note: To highlight text, place your cursor at the beginning section. While holding down the <**SHIFT**> key, use the arrow keys to highlight. This gives more control than using a mouse or touchpad.

Note: To delete a section, place the cursor at the beginning of the text and select all up to and including the section break. Once highlighted, press the <**DEL**> key.

3.4. Headers

A Trade Paperback has a convention that the Author's Name is on the top of even pages (left) and the title of the book is on odd pages (right), not counting the first page of a chapter or title pages. This would be exceptionally tedious if you typed in each and every one. Instead, there is the option of setting up **Headers**, which can be configured to be different on odd, even and first pages. These apply to **Sections** (remember we talked about **Sections** having the ability to possess different formatting? This is one place it comes into play.)

Since this project began with the templates from CreateSpace, the headers are already configured. Notice the grayed text at the top of each non-first page (**Figure 20**). On the left, is **AUTHOR NAME**, on the right is **TITLE**. Double click on either field and then fill in ***Your Name*** in place of **AUTHOR NAME** and the ***Book Title*** in place of **TITLE**. To return to the main manuscript field, double click anywhere in the body of the text.

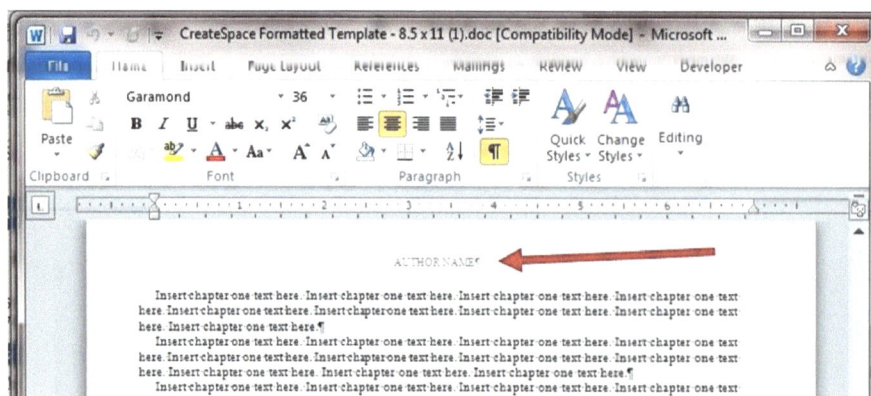

Figure 20. CS—Headers

To see how the headers are configured, navigate to the <**Page Layout**> toolbar and click on <**Page Setup**>. Clicking on the <**Layout**> tab reveals the header configuration(**Figure 21**).

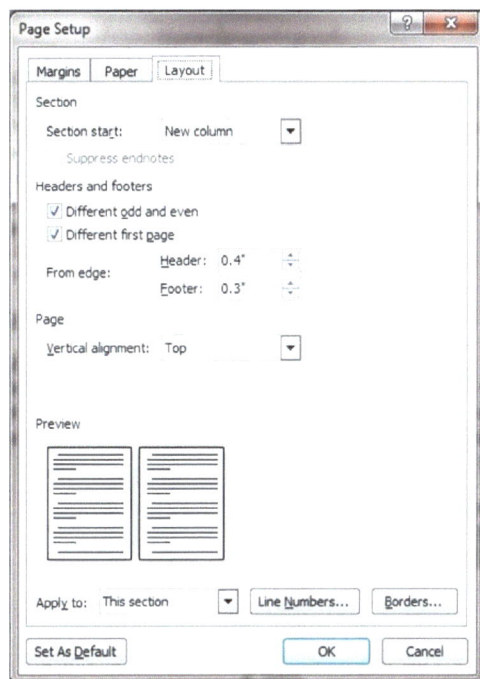

Figure 21. CS—Header Dialogue

3.5.   Chapter Content

3.5.1. Paragraph Formatting

The first step in formatting the manuscript is to understand **what** the formatting is. Some of the information is easy to find, some, not so much. The next few steps are focused on finding, understanding and saving the formatting so it can be duplicated or modified as desired.

1. Scroll down to the first *indented* paragraph of Chapter 1 in the working file. This should be the second paragraph.
2. Right click anywhere in the paragraph and select <**Paragraph**> in the drop down menu. The settings in the pop up display should resemble that in **Figure 22**.

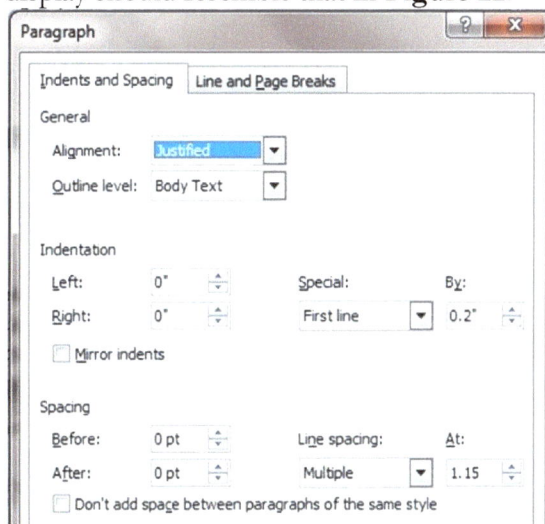

Figure 22. CS—Paragraph Formatting

3. Write down the settings indicated in **Figure 22** (*Alignment*, all fields in *Indentation* and *Spacing*, *Special* and *Line spacing*). These will be used in the next steps.

3.5.2. Copying and Formatting Original Text

Note: When working with the two files, make sure the original file is not modified and saved. This is to ensure there is a copy that can always be recovered if sections are inadvertently deleted or distorted. <**UNDO**> is your friend!!!

1. Open the original manuscript and highlight the Chapter 1 text.
2. Right click in the highlighted area and select <**Copy**> in the drop down menu.
3. Return to the working file and highlight all the text in Chapter 1, making sure not to include the final <**End of Section**> marker.
4. Right click in the highlighted area; select <**Paste**> from the drop down menu.
5. At this point, the text from the original manuscript should appear in place of the canned text from the template.
6. Highlight the entire text in Chapter 1 (working file) up to and not including the <**End of Section**> marker.
7. Right click in the highlighted area and select <**Paragraph**> from the drop down menu.
8. Fill in all parameters as recorded in steps **3.5.1, 2&3**.
9. Highlight the text in the first paragraph up to and including the paragraph marker (**Figure 23-1**).

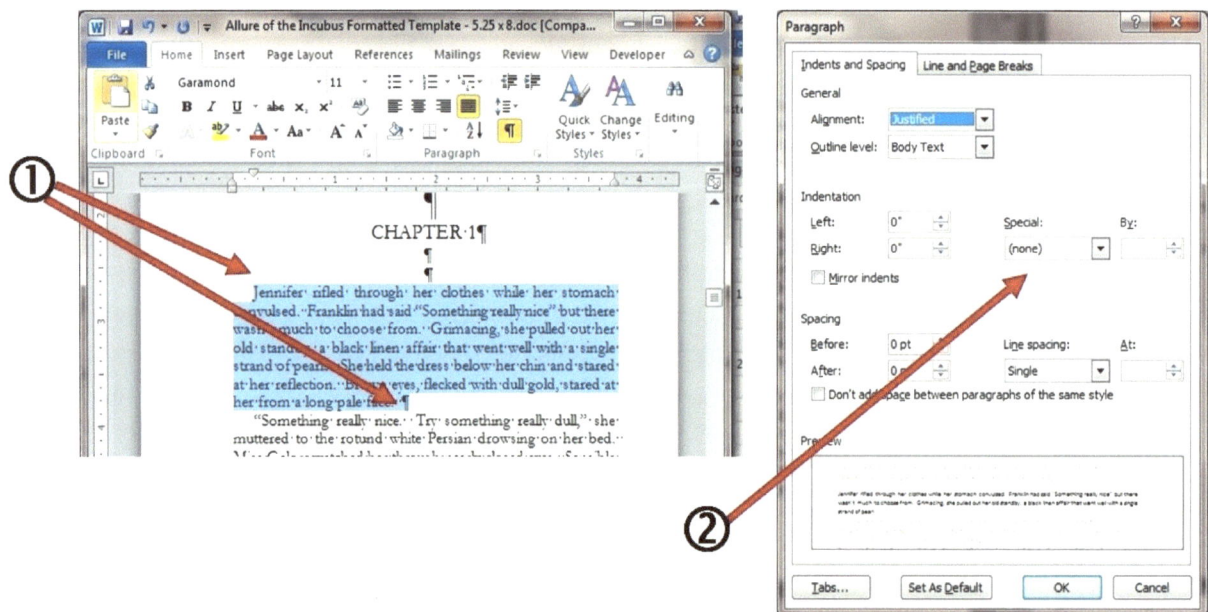

Figure 23. C9—First Paragraph Formatting / First Line Indentation

10. Right click anywhere in the highlighted area and select <**Paragraph**> from the drop down menu.
11. Remove the First Line indention by selecting <**none**> from the drop down menu under <**Special**> (**Figure 23-2**) and click <**OK**>.
12. First paragraph should resemble the formatting in **Figure 24**.
13. Repeat steps **3.5.2, 1-12** for all chapters.

Note: All content from Chapter 1 to the end of the book can be copy and pasted as one section, but verify that the first page of each chapter hasn't been distorted. If in doubt, do one chapter at a time until comfortable with the process.

Note: Traditional print format has the first paragraph with no indentation and all subsequent paragraphs indented. If there are a lot of graphics, do what looks reasonable.

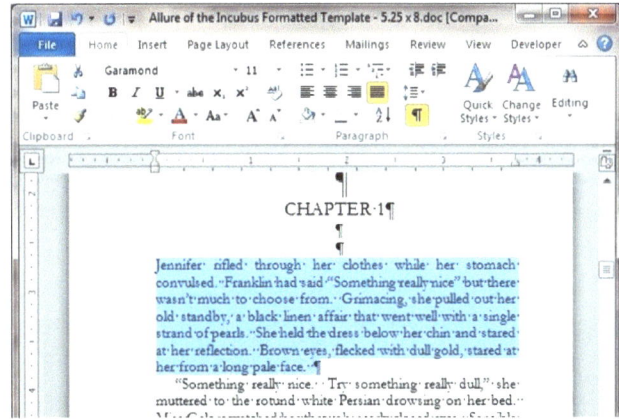

Figure 24. CS—First Paragraph Indentation Removed

3.5.3. Chapter Headings

1. Navigate to the beginning of each chapter.
2. Highlight the Chapter Information (Chapter Title and Number).
3. Right click in the highlighted area.
4. Select <**Font**> from the drop down menu.
5. Ensure the <**All caps**> selection (**Figure 25-①**) is unchecked; click <**OK**>. <**All caps**> appears to simplify formatting, but complicates TOC and other actions.

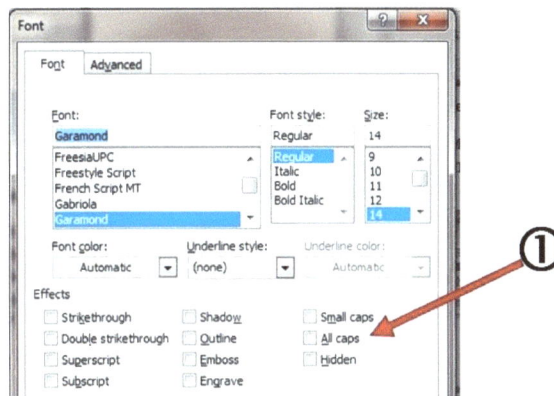

Figure 25. CS—Deselect <All Caps> in Chapter Headings

6. Type the Chapter Information in all caps if desired, or format appropriately.
7. Highlight the Chapter Information and click <**Heading 1**> from the toolbar (**Figure 26-1**).

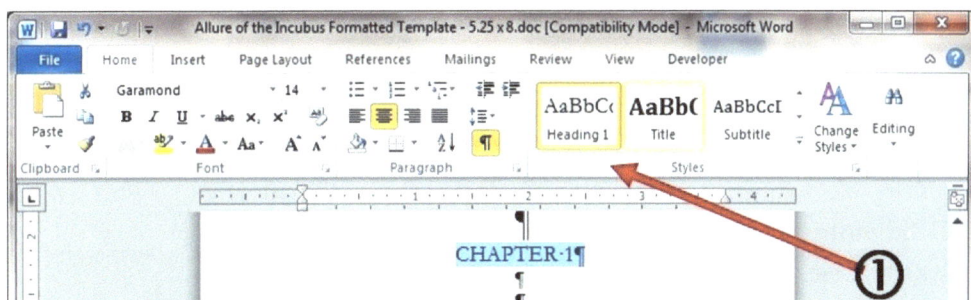

Figure 26. CS—Chapter Information to Heading 1

8. If the <**Heading 1**> settings differ from the font desired for the chapter headings, they can be modified. If they don't require modification, skip to the next step.
9. Highlight the Chapter Information.
10. Right click anywhere in the highlighted area
11. Select <**Font**> from the drop down menu.
12. Modify the font as desired and click <**OK**>.
13. Center align using the toolbar (**Figure 27-1**)
14. Place your cursor anywhere in the chapter verbiage and number.
15. Right click on the <**Heading 1**> selection on the top toolbar (**Figure 27-2**).
16. Click on <**Update Heading to Match Selection**>.

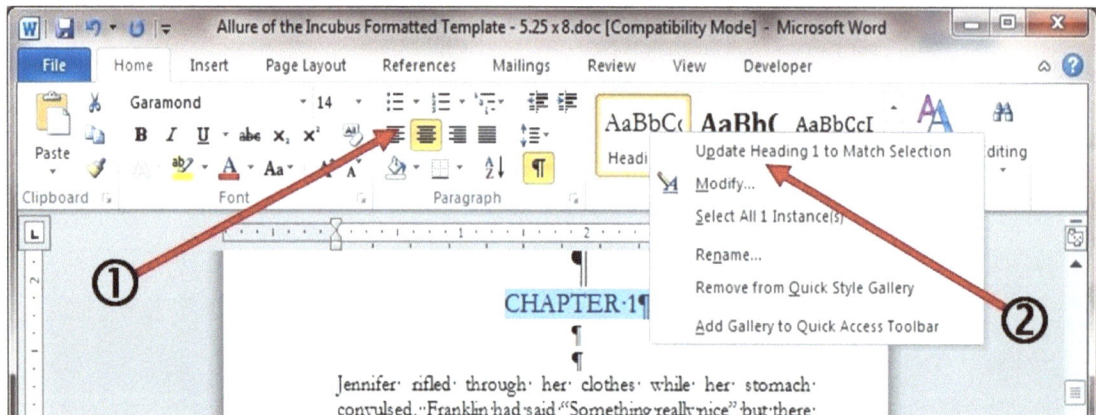

Figure 27. CS—Update Heading 1 to Match Selection

17. Repeat steps **3.5.3, 1-7** for each chapter. Steps **8-15** only have to be performed once.

3.6. Graphics (Optional)

Creating a Graphic Novel or a Children's Picture Book is beyond the scope of this handbook, but both could be attempted using the steps in this section. The actual artwork is assumed to exist; that is, it has been created outside of Word® with whatever tools the artist prefers. Once created, graphics files such as JPG, PNG or GIFs must be available (default for an eBook is either JPG or TIFF; my preference is JPG). There is some minor manipulation necessary, but will be accomplished with the freeware program *Paint*. Others can be used, but this is my application of choice. Mainly because it's readily available, easy to use, and *free*.

3.6.1. Preparing the Graphics Files

All Print Ready graphics must be a minimum of 300 DPI (Dots Per Inch) or CreateSpace will squawk. I have included graphics with the Windows system default of 96 DPI and they have printed just fine, but the higher resolution will print better. Higher than 300 DPI for most books is overkill and will only bloat the size of the finished book.

Any screen capture, imports or cut and paste will default to 96 DPI, but there are some tricks for forcing the 300 DPI. The first step is to find an image, a JPG, with a 300 DPI. It doesn't matter what it is, just scout around on the Internet or visit my webpage. I have samples files there if you'd like to grab one of them. Once the image is stored, right click on the file and click on <**Properties**>. This will report the DPI. Ensure it is 300 DPI before moving on to the next steps.

1. Right click on the file and select <**Open With**> then <**Paint**>.
2. Once in Paint, click on the file icon at the top (**Figure 28-1**), then <**Properties**>, and verify the DPI (**Figure 28**).

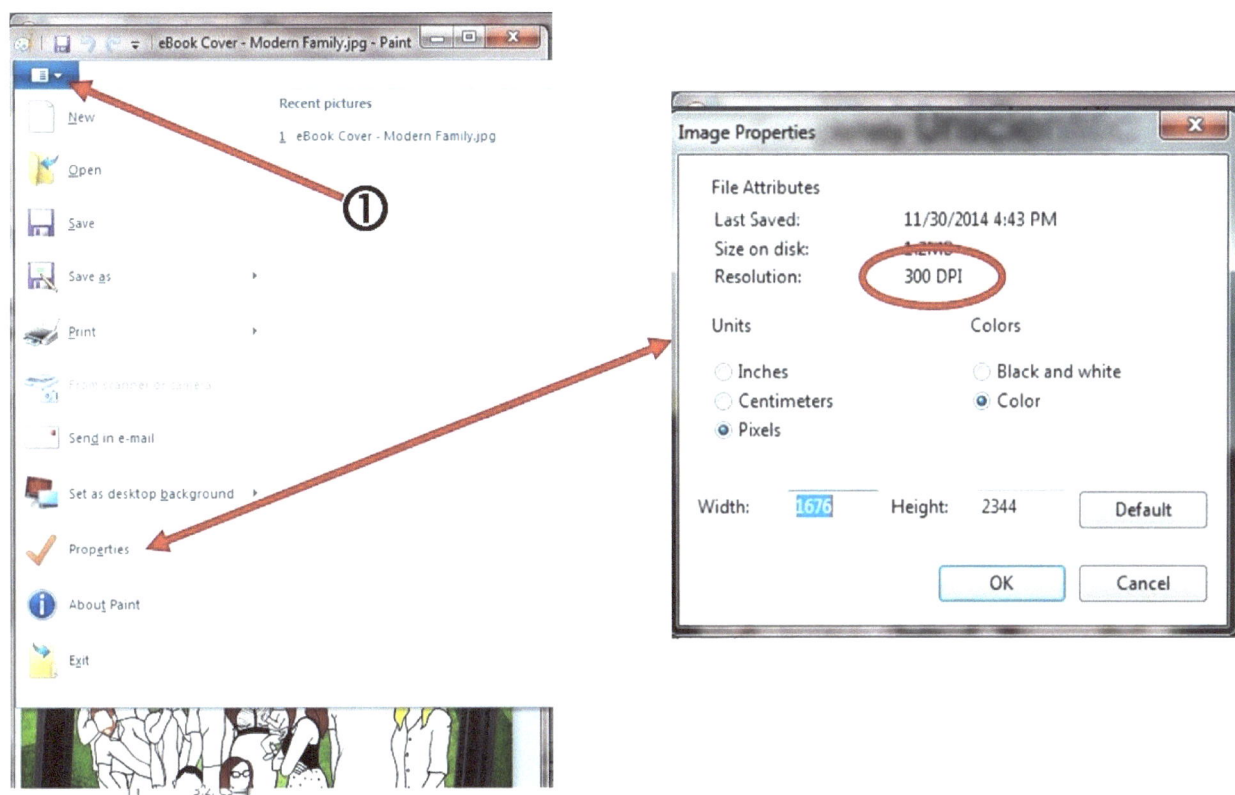

Figure 28. Verify Image DPI with Paint

3. Close this dialog window, returning to the main screen of Paint. Leave Paint open, i.e. do not close the file, and navigate to the folder containing the file you wish to manipulate.

4. Right click on the desired file and select <**Open With**> then <**Paint**>. There should now be two instances of Paint open.

5. Check the DPI of the desired file. If it's 300 DPI or more, you're done and can move on to section **3.6.2 Inserting Graphics Files**. If not, continue on to step 6.

6. Click anywhere in the desired graphic and press <**CTRL**><**A**> (case insensitive, 'a' or 'A' work). This selects the entire or 'All' graphic.

7. Click the <**Copy**> icon at the top, right click and select <**Copy**> from the drop down menu, or press <**CTRL**><**C**>. All are ways to copy a selected area.

8. Navigate to the other instance of Paint, the one with the 300 DPI image.

9. Click anywhere in this graphic and click the <**Paste**> icon at the top, right click and select <**Paste**> from the drop down menu, or press <**CTRL**><**V**>. All are ways to paste from the Clipboard.

10. At this point, your 'new' image is overlaid on top of the high resolution image. Zoom in or out until both images are completely visible and there is some empty space around both (**Figure 29**).

11. Press <**ESC**> to deselect the images and zoom in on the sizing handles (**Figure 29**).

12. Position the cursor over a sizing handle (outermost edge of the larger image), press and hold the left mouse key and drag the handle in until the previous image is no longer visible.

13. Be careful not to cut off any of the desired image. If you overshoot, click on <**UNDO**>. Remember your friend!

Note: If the image appears to stretch, the copied image was still selected when the handle was dragged. Click <**UNDO**>, which should cause the image to snap back out. Click on <**ESC**> until the image is no longer selected (no dashed line around the graphic) and then drag the outer handle again.

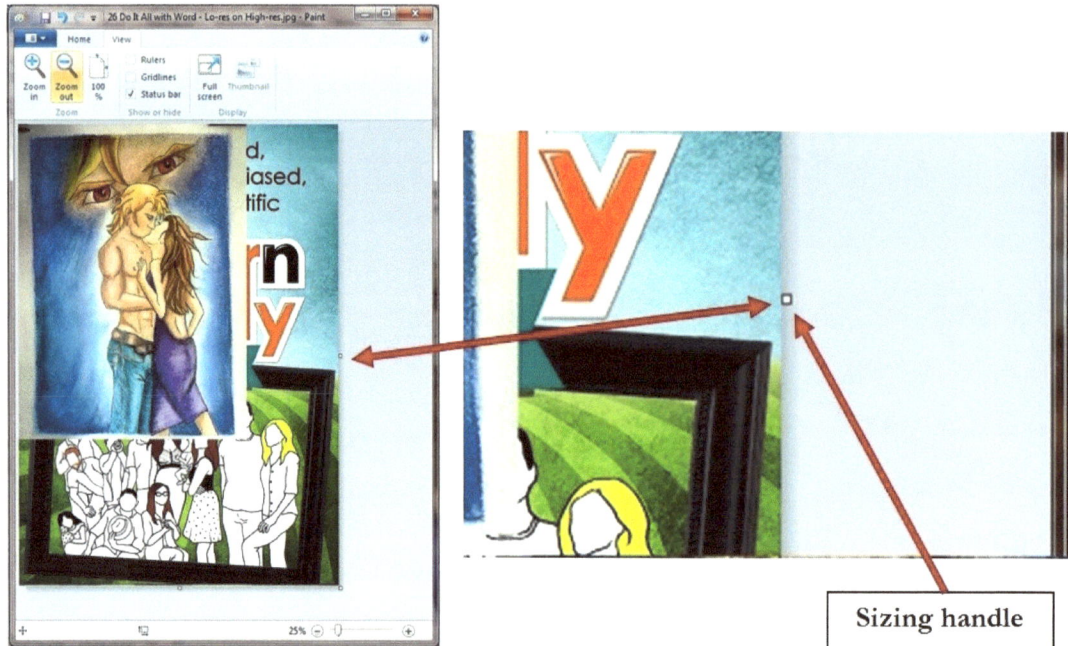

Figure 29. Paint—Low Resolution Image Overlaid on High Resolution Image

14. Once the image is cleaned up to your satisfaction, click on the <**File**> icon and select <**Save As**>. Save the image as a JPG in the folder of your choice. Don't forget to give it a meaningful name.

3.6.2. Inserting Graphics Files

Once a file is at least 300 DPI, it can be inserted into the manuscript with the following steps.

1. Open the manuscript and navigate to the desired page.
2. With the Formatting Marks on, press <**Enter**> several times. Exact amount isn't important, but give yourself some room to work with (**Figure 30**).
3. Position the cursor at the beginning of one of the blank lines and select <**Insert**> at the top tool bar. Once the <**Insert**> toolbar is visible, click on <**Picture**> (**Figure 30**).

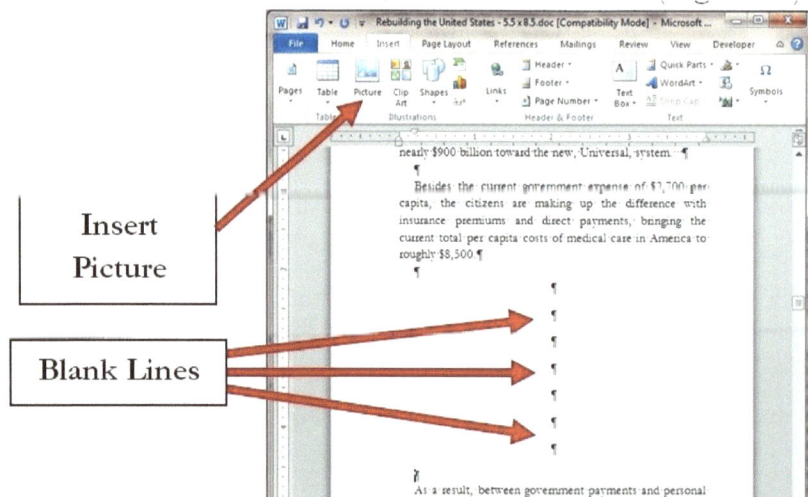

Figure 30. CS—Empty Lines Preparing for <Insert Picture> - <In Front of Text>

4. Once you click on <**Picture**>, a browse window will open. Navigate to the desired graphics file,

click on it and then press <**Enter**> or <**OK**>.

5. The picture is now in the manuscript. Right click on the image and select <**Format Picture**>. The menu in **Figure 31** will appear. Click on <**Layout**>.

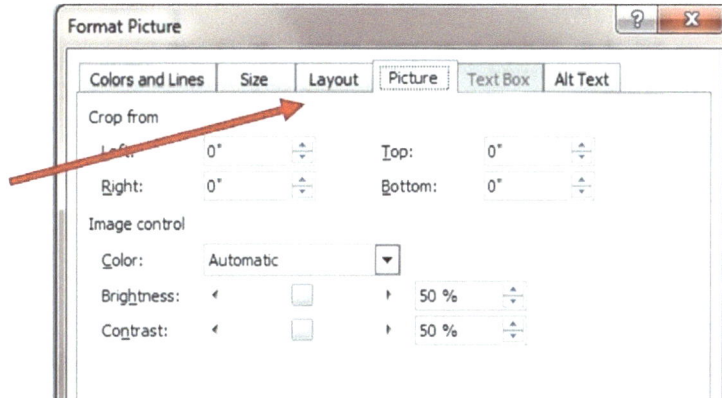

Figure 31. CS—Format Picture

6. The default is <**In line with text**> (**Figure 32-1**), which is also the formatting necessary for an eBook. To center the image, navigate to the <**Home**> tab and click on the center alignment. If the graphic is situated the way you'd like it, remove the extra blank lines and move on to the next step. This formatting selection means that the image is dependent on the text in the document. An alternative is to click on <**In Front of text**> (**Figure 32-2**), which allows the image to 'float' – this is where the blank lines become important. Press <**Enter**> or <**OK**>. Now you can drag and drop the image wherever you want. Add more blank lines if the area isn't big enough. Also, you can select the sizing handles and change the size of the image to accommodate the document. <**Square**> or <**Tight**> allows you to place the text to either side of the text, if you want to have sidebars or images that are to the side of your text.

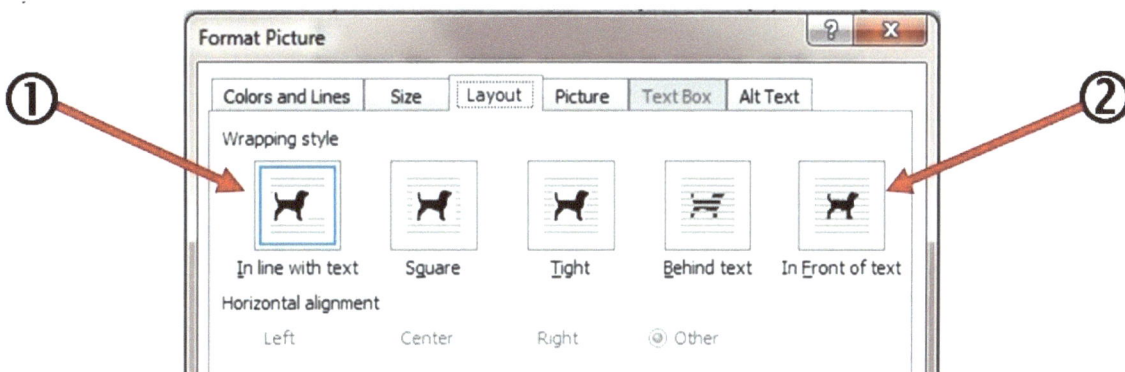

Figure 32. CS—Format Picture - Layout

Note: When an image is selected, the <**Picture Tools**> toolbar appears at the top of the working area. This toolbar duplicates the drop down menu and can be used directly instead of the right click process.

Note: To reach a larger market, it's important to have both an eBook and a paperback. Since eBooks control the formatting and layout, <**In line with text**> is the preferred image formatting. To avoid having radically different manuscripts for the two media, use this option whenever possible.

3.6.3. Adding Captions (Optional)

Not all images require captions, but they can be useful for non-fiction or How-To books (like this one!).

Allowing Word® to generate the captions means they can be automatically updated and remove the need to manually keep track of numbering. They are also necessary to create an automatic **List of Figures**.

1. Enter a blank line below the image.
2. Click on <**References**> (**Figure 33**) on the upper toolbar.
3. Once the <**References**> toolbar appears, click on <**Insert Caption**>(**Figure 33**). The dialogue box in **Figure 34** will appear.

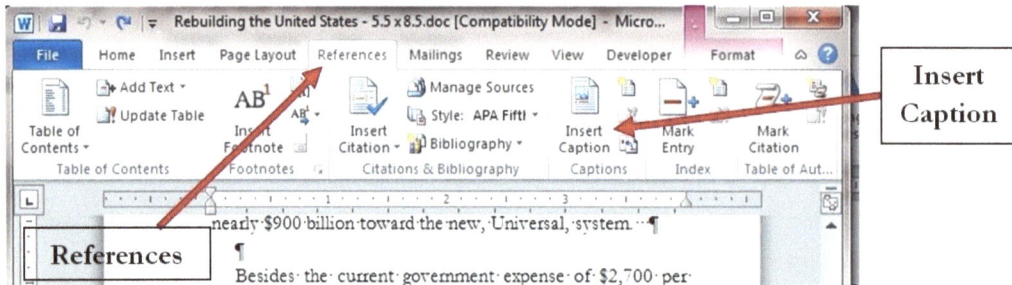

Figure 33. CS—References Toolbar

4. The label **Figure x** will be preloaded into the appropriate field. Enter the desired text and click <**Enter**> or <**OK**>. You can also use the drop down menu to name a **Table**, change the numbering format, the label or any other field in this menu.

Note: Adjust the way **Captions** look by opening the **Styles** dialogue box, navigate to **Captions**, right click and select **Modify**. This avoids having to modify every caption to center, bold, italics, etc.

Note: If **Center Alignment** is chosen for a caption, when the **Insert Caption** dialogue box opens, the label/number won't appear because it's off the screen. Either type without seeing the text and correct any mistakes afterwards, or select **Left Alignment** and center each caption after clicking **OK**.

Note: The **Insert Caption** dialogue entry is necessary for an *automatic* **List of Figures** or **Tables**.

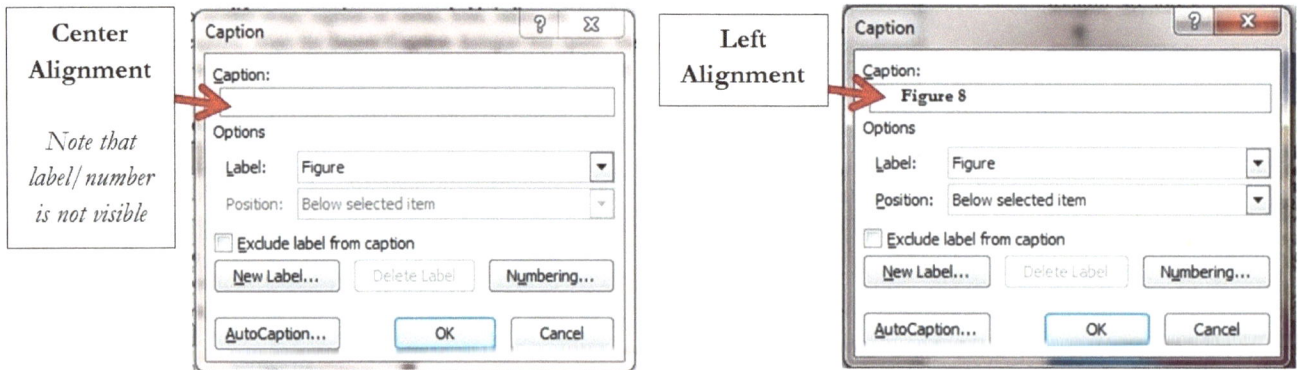

Figure 34. CS—Insert Caption for Figures or Tables

3.7. Table of Contents and List of Figures (Optional)

While not mandatory, some books benefit from a **Table of Contents (TOC)**, a **List of Figures** and / or a **List of Tables**. Manually entering these can be tedious and error-prone, but if automatic styles are used for **Headings** and **Captions**, the lists can be updated automatically.

TOC:

1. Just after the **Dedication** and before **Acknowledgements**, there's a section entitled **Contents**. Delete the table and title, up to, but not including the **Section Break**. If it's already been deleted,

insert two **Page Break**s to ensure the TOC begins on an odd page.

2. Click on the tab at the top of the document entitled <**References**>.

3. Click on the <**Table of Contents**> icon. Select the format you like best and click on it. The TOC will now be centered on the page. If you don't like the look of it, click <**UNDO**> and try another format or scroll to the bottom and click on <**Insert Table of Contents**> for a custom table.

4. From now on, whenever you put in a new heading or add more pages, navigate back to the TOC, right click in the headings area and select <**Update Field**>. When the pop-up menu asks if you want to <**Update page numbers only**> or <**Update entire table**>, select <**Update entire table**>. Seriously, why not? Better safe than sorry.

List of Figures / Tables:

1. Navigate to the **TOC**. Form dictates that you shouldn't have a **List of Figures / Tables** if you don't have a **TOC**.

2. Ensure there is a blank page (<**Insert**><**Page Break**>)after the TOC, so that each list is on an odd page. Position your cursor on the first blank odd page after the TOC.

3. Click on the tab at the top of the document entitled <**References**>.

4. Click on the <**Insert List of Figures**> icon and the dialogue box in **Figure 35** appears.

5. The field labeled <**Caption Label**> (**Figure 35-2**) dictates what kind of list you're inserting. Default is <**Figure**>, other choices are <**Equation**> and <**Table**>. It is acceptable to have all three, they just need to be entered one at a time.

6. Select the format you like best (**Figure 35-1**) and click on it. The List of Figures will now be centered on the page. If you don't like the look of it, click <**UNDO**> and try another format.

7. Update this List just as you would the TOC.

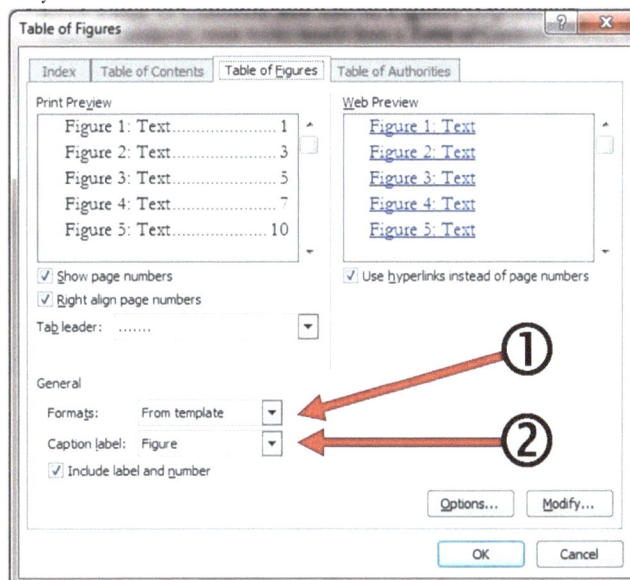

Figure 35. CS—List of Figures / Tables Dialogue Box

3.8. Changing Trim Size

What happens if you complete your interior formatting and decide the trim size should be changed? Do you have to start over? Throw yourself off a building? Not at all! It's straightforward to change the size.

1. Navigate to <**Page Layout**>, then select <**Size**> and <**More Paper Sizes**>. The dialogue box in **Figure 36** will appear.

2. Fill in the <**Width**> and <**Height**> (**Figure 36-1**). Note that the <**Paper Size**> at the top of the

dialogue box may change to <**Custom Size**> (**Figure 36-2**) if the new size isn't standard.

3. After <**Apply to**>, select <**Whole Document**> in the drop down selections (**Figure 36-3**).
4. Click <**OK**>.
5. Examine the document to ensure all images, paragraphs, headings, etc. line up properly.

Note: I highly recommend renaming the document to reflect the new trim size. I.e. "*file 5x8*.docx" or "*file 5.25x8.41*.docx". Embedded dots are okay in a file name.

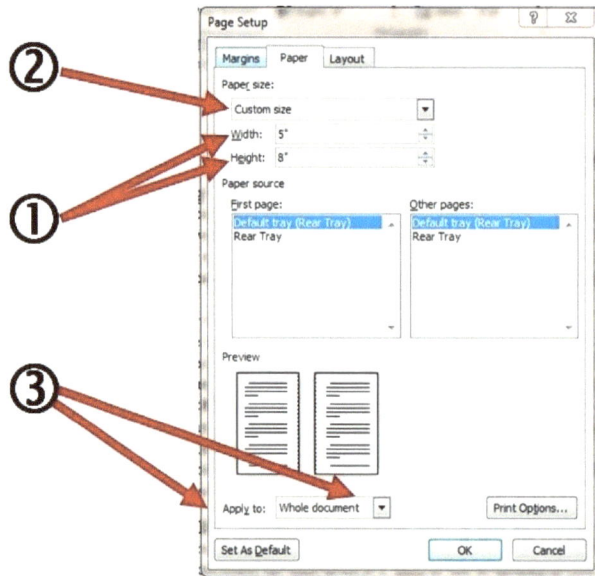

Figure 36. CS—Paper Size (Trim Size) Modification

3.9. Portable Document Format (PDF)

To submit your manuscript, it must be Print Ready, which means it must be a PDF.

1. Ensure the document has been saved as a .docx or .doc as dictated by your version of Word®.
2. Click on the <**File**> tab at the top of the document.
3. On the drop down menu, select <**Save As**>.
4. When the browser dialogue appears(**Figure 37**), click on the drop down area beside the field <**Save as Type:**> (**Figure 37-1**) and select <**PDF (*.pdf)**> (**Figure 38-1**).
5. (Optional but good idea) Click on the blue fields <**Authors**> and <**Title**> (**Figure 37-2**)and replace the existing content with your information.
6. Ensure the title is correct (it should duplicate the book title or CreateSpace will squawk) and is in the correct folder and select <**Save**>.

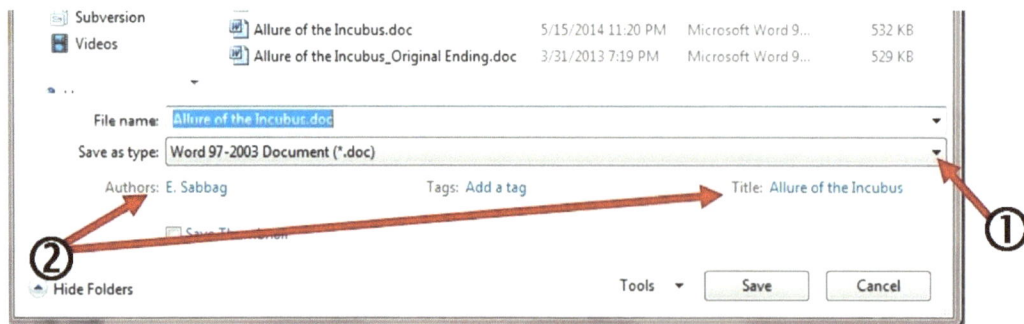

Figure 37. CS—Save As Dialogue Box

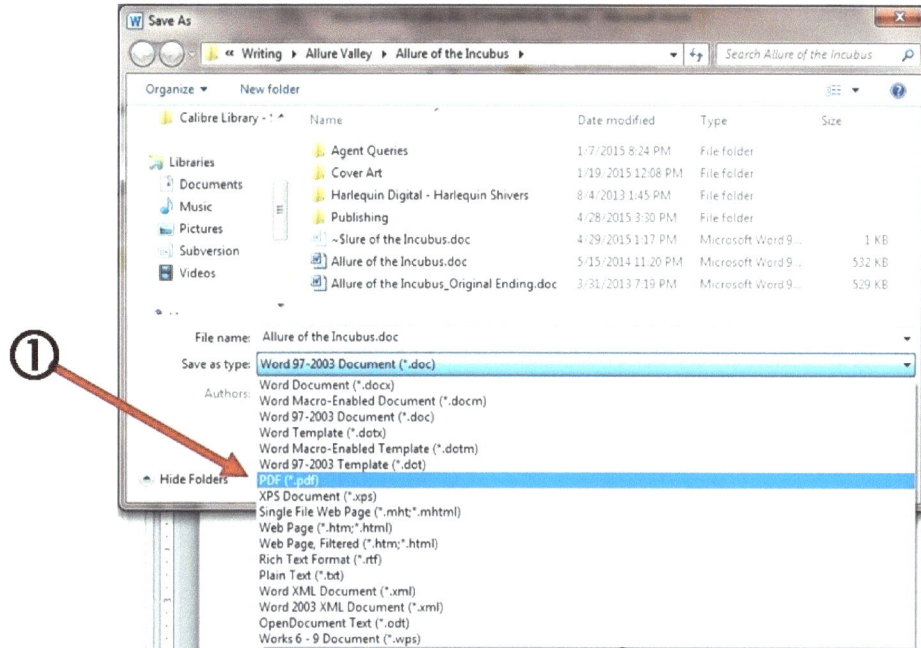

Figure 38. CS—Save As Dialogue Box - PDF

3.10. Summation

A tremendous amount of information has been presented in this chapter and it may seem daunting. However, it's presented in a sequential fashion in the hope that you can follow it step by step to format your book. Take it one section at a time and, before you know it, you will have a Print Ready manuscript ready to be submitted to CreateSpace. And that's one step closer to having a published novel that you can be proud of!

Chapter 4.**CS—Cover Art**

4.1. Obtaining the Artwork

A big mistake I made on my first self-published novel was that the cover art was an afterthought. All my attention was spent on the content, which is, of course, extremely important, and I assumed that I could cruise the web, find some images, knit them together and POOF! Magic. A book cover. As I hope you're thinking, turns out there are issues with copyrighting, getting the correct resolution, avoiding a Franken-picture and realizing your vision. When I realized all this and accepted that I am not a graphics artist, I turned to Cover Creator. Which produced an exceptionally blah, truly boring, cookie cutter cover. In a panic, I scrambled to find an artist, which I did, through the help of some friends. A truly talented individual, she has created some lovely cover art, which is unique to my books. However, she's not in the business of churning out book covers and has a life. As a result, it's difficult to prevail upon her with too many demands. This was a problem. Then, I attended a writers' conference where a speaker introduced me to **99Designs** (https://99designs.com/). As mentioned previously, quality artwork is one of the areas I believe should be delegated and should be paid for. Don't promise a friend a portion of the royalties. Seriously. Don't do it.

There are similar websites, but this particular site is the one I enjoy the most. The costs are reasonable, the designs transcend what I can imagine and they refund your money if you don't receive a good design. There are some codicils to keep in mind:

1. Be clear and detailed when setting up your contest, but don't constrain the artists too much.
2. Global contests mean language barriers. Give as much visual direction as you can.
3. Be actively involved – the more feedback, the better.
4. When you're assessing the designs, think about the image as a thumbnail. Most books are featured online and you want the design to pop.
5. Polls are useful tools, but the final decision is yours. I've had designers skew the results to imply their design is favored.
6. Request at least 300 DPI and RGB (Red/Green/Blue). CMYK (Cyan/Magenta/Yellow/Key-Black) is acceptable, but not well interpreted by Word® and RGB is a good compromise for both print and the web (thumbnails on online stores and eBooks).
7. Once the final design is selected, ensure you have the complete cover, front, spine and back, before releasing payment.
8. Nail down the trim size before starting the contest. A design created for 5"x8" may not adjust properly for 8.5"x11" and possibly even look distorted.
9. For the back cover, make sure there are spaces for the ISBN block, author's photo, and verbiage. Shy away from a cluttered design on the back—this is advertising / marketing space and you don't want to waste it. If the artist has included this information as a place holder, have them remove it.

4.2. Working with the Cover Template

Whether you contract with an artist or create the artwork yourself, this section assumes you have an image file suitable for the cover art. The challenge is making it print ready. Again, CreateSpace supplies the necessary templates.

1. Navigate to the Project Homepage as discussed in section **2.6 Project Homepage.**
2. On the sidebar, click on <**How to make a cover PDF**> (**Figure 39-1**).

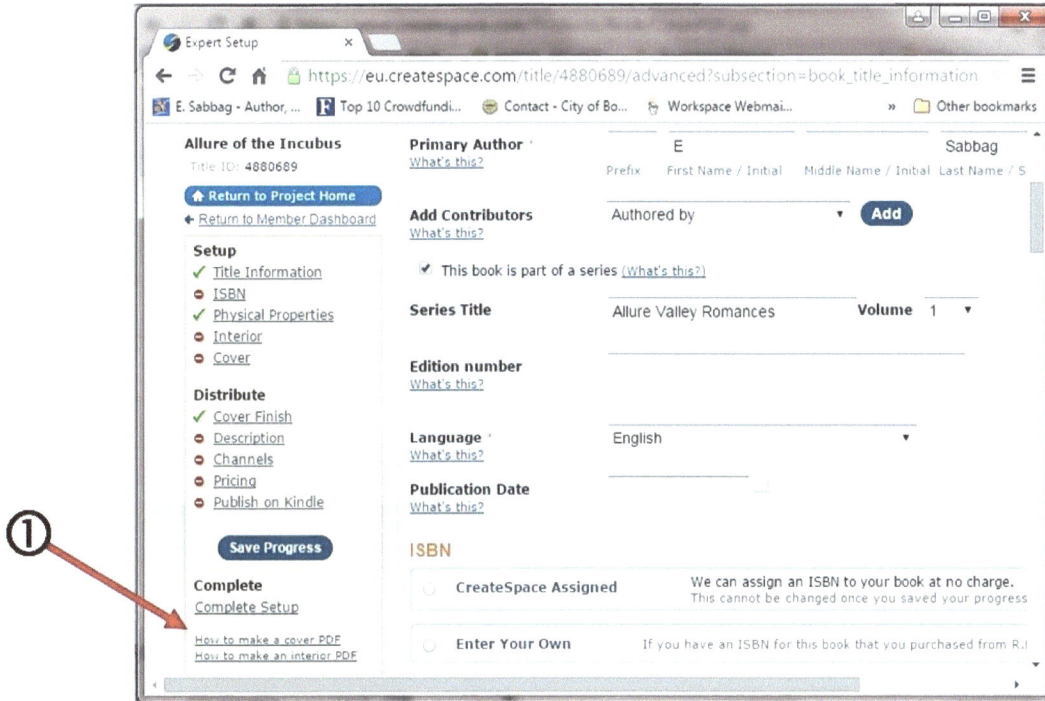

Figure 39. CS—How to Make a Cover PDF

3. On the resulting page, there is a LOT of information on how to calculate the size of the cover based on trim size, type of paper, number of pages and so on. However. This is CreateSpace and they give excellent templates. Scroll down to <**Get a head start with one of our cover templates**> and click on <**Download Cover Templates**> (**Figure 40-1**).

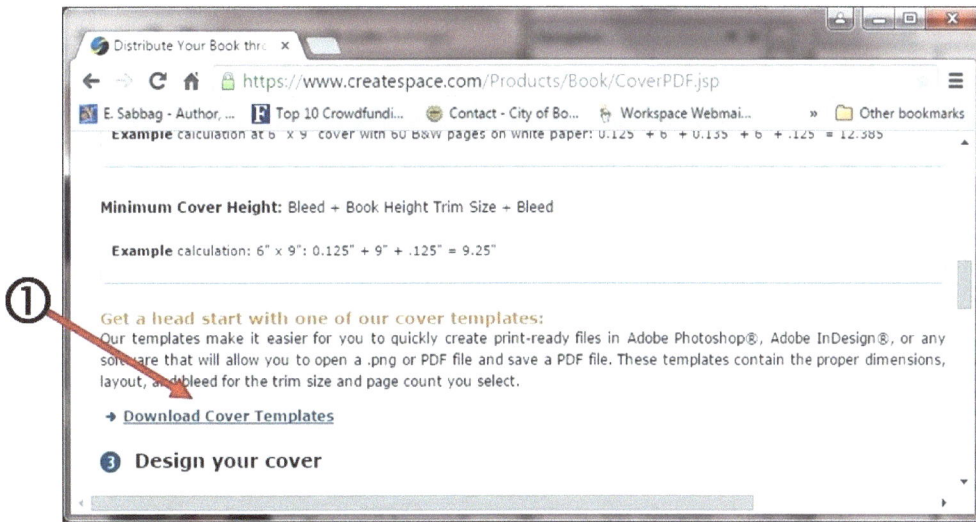

Figure 40. CS—How to Make a Cover PDF - Download Template

4. Fill in the information that correlates to your book in the <**Configure your Template**> area (**Figure 41-1**).
5. Click on <**Build Template**>(**Figure 41-2**).

Note: If an error message appears saying a template isn't available for the chosen size, select a template similar in size and it can be adjusted for your project.

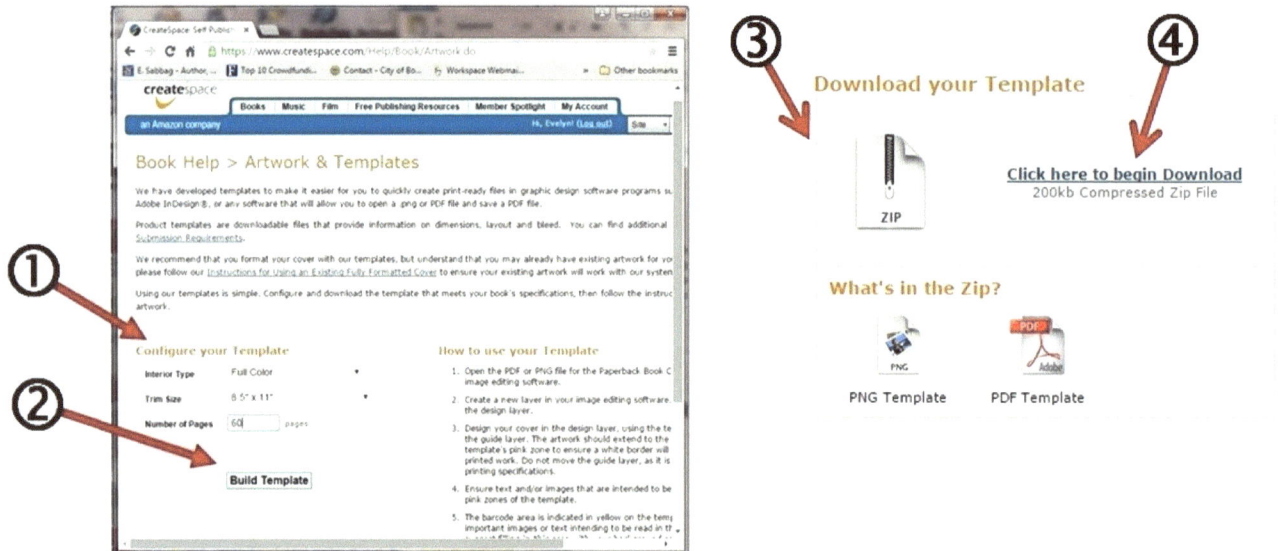

Figure 41. CS—Configure Your (Cover) Template

6. On the resulting screen (**Figure 41-3**), click on <**Click here to begin Download**> **Figure 41-4)** and copy the resulting zip file to the Templates folder created in section **2.3 PC Folder Structure.**
7. Unzip the files. There should be a PDF and a PNG (Portable Network Graphics) version of the template.
8. Open the PNG file with Paint. The image will be very large, so you may have to zoom WAAAAY out to see it (<**View**> and <**Zoom**> or slider bar at the lower right hand corner. Once you can see the entire image, it may resemble **Figure 42**.

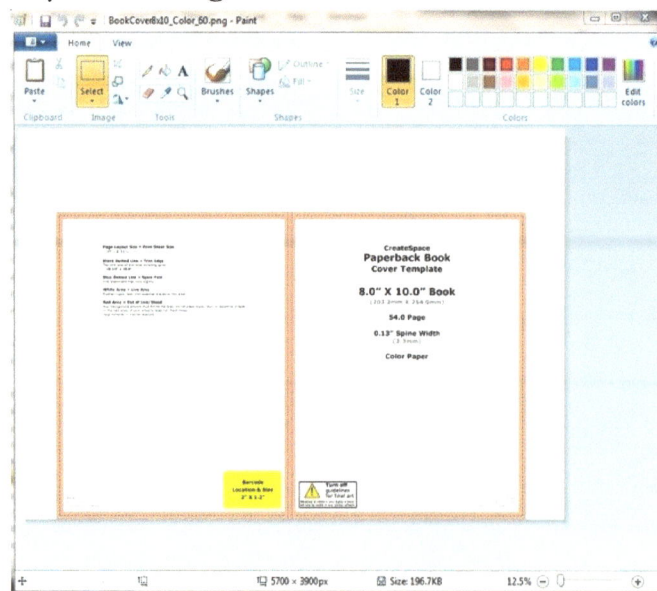

Figure 42. CS—Cover Template PNG

9. For ease of use, the white area all around the pink frame should be trimmed. To trim it, click <**ESC**> to deselect the entire image.

10. Click on <**Select**> on the top toolbar.

11. Place the cursor at the upper left hand corner of the pink frame. Holding down the left mouse button, *drag* the dotted rectangle to the lower right hand corner of the pink frame, making sure to include ALL the pink and leaving no white. It may take a few tries, but it gets easier with practice.

12. With a dotted line around the entire pink frame, click <**CTRL**> <**X**> (cut). The pink frame should completely disappear. Note that the image is being *cut* rather than ***dragged*** to avoid distortion.

13. Place the cursor in the uppermost left corner of the Paint working area. Type <**CTRL**> <**V**> (paste). The frame should now be positioned in the upper left hand corner of the working area. While it is still selected, it can be moved around with your mouse until it is positioned correctly.

14. Using the technique described in section **3.6.1 Preparing the Graphics Files, step 11**, remove the extraneous white area. The resulting image should be a rectangle completely framed in pink.

15. Perform a <**Save As**> and save the image as a **JPG** to the **Cover Art** folder created in section **PC Folder Structure.**

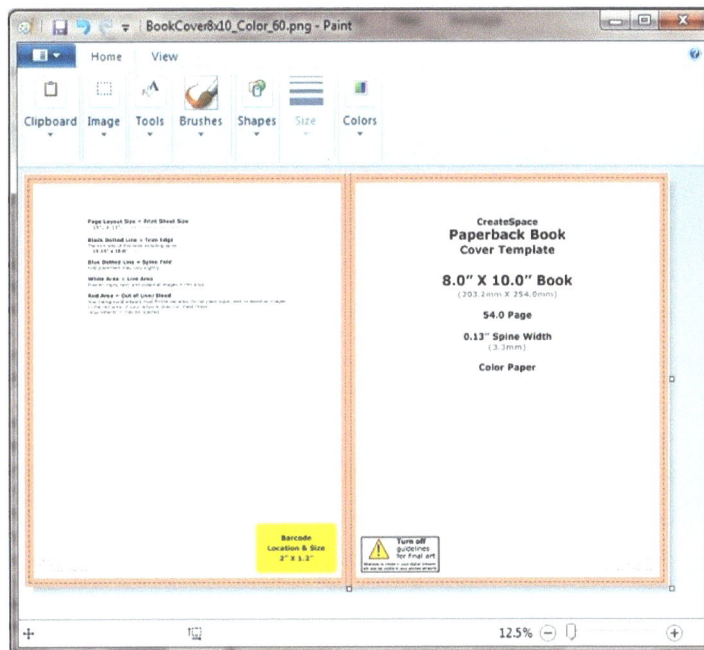

Figure 43. CS—Cover Template JPG

This is a good time to examine the template. All the information necessary is printed on the image. The pink area is for ***bleed***. That is, when the cover is actually printed, there is an amount of uncertainty in the final product. The pink area is that uncertainty. The image selected for the book should completely cover this area, but not contain anything important as it could be cut off. This example is too narrow for verbiage on the spine, so the entire spine is pink. The yellow rectangle is the barcode area, which will be filled in by CreateSpace. Again, do not put anything in this area that you care about being covered up.

4.3. Fitting the Image to a Document

For the project in this example, there wasn't a template available for the exact size (8.5"x11"). As a result, I'll explain how to adapt the 8"x10" template for this project. Unfortunately for anyone math averse, there is some math involved. Fortunately, it's easy.

1. Open a blank document in Word®. Save it as ***Name of Book – Cover.docx (doc)*** in the cover art folder.

2. This will be a custom sized document. If you were able to download a template for your project, read the values off the upper left hand corner of the template and skip to step 8. Else, calculate the trim size via the following steps. Note that the values comes from the page described in section **4.2 Working with the Cover Template, step 3** (the stuff I said you didn't need. Now you need it).

3. The spine width is dictated by the number of ALL pages (read off the bottom left hand corner of your document) times the paper width (0.002252 for white, 0.0025 for cream) and an additional multiplier of 0.002347 for full color interior. Black and white interior does not require a multiplier.

4. For the complete cover width (back, front and spine), add the book's trim size, bleed (0.125") and spine. Remember that bleed and the trim width must be multiplied by two (front and back).

5. For the height, add the trim height and 2 x bleed.

6. For the example project (8.5"x11", 65 pages, full color interior, white paper), the width is: 0.125"+8.5"+65*0.002347"+8.5" + 0.125" = 17.402555, rounded down to **17.40"**.

7. The example project height is: 0.125" + 0.125" + 11 = **11.25"**

8. In the new document navigate to the size dialogue and enter the calculated width and height or the values read off the template. Save the document (section **3.8 Changing Trim Size**).

Note: The trim size does not have to be exact. As long as it's close, CreateSpace will adjust the uploaded file to fit the book. Proofing the book will determine whether or not the adjustment looks correct.

Now that the document is created and saved, the next sections will fit the template image and the design image(s) to the document. Ensuring the document is the correct size makes fitting the images easier.

1. Open the Cover document and zoom out until the entire document can be seen. Depending on your monitor size, this should be around 50% or so.

2. Click anywhere in the working area and insert the template JPG using <**Insert**> <**Picture**>.

3. Format the picture with <**Wrap Text**> <**In Front of Text**>. This allows the image to *float*.

4. Ensure the image is selected by clicking anywhere on the image. Using a combination of stretching (sizing handles, left mouse key and dragging or <**Picture Tools**> <**Width/Height**> fields) and dragging the image (left mouse key or arrow keys), fill the white space completely. The aspect ratio should be unclicked for these operations (<**Picture Tools**> <**Size**> <**lock aspect ratio**> field). The result should resemble **Figure 44**.

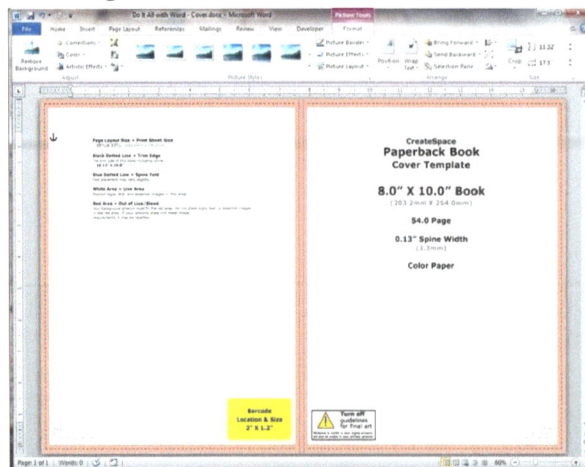

Figure 44. CS—Properly Positioned Template Image

5. SAVE THIS FILE. A lot of work has been accomplished and you don't want to lose it.

The next steps position the design image and verbiage onto the template. This requires working back and forth to determine the correct placement, which makes use of <**Ordering**>. Think of the images as a series of transparent slides, all stacked exactly on top of each other. You control which one is on top (front) and which one is on the bottom (back). The final design will completely obscure the template image, but it will remain in the file for reference. The required dialogue box is accessed by selecting an image and then right clicking. From the drop down menu, select <**Bring to Front**> (**Figure 45-1**) or <**Send to Back**> (**Figure 45-2**) as desired. Note that there is a <**Bring Forward**> / <**Send Backward**> in the <**Picture Tools**> toolbar (**Figure 45-3**), but these have unpredictable results.

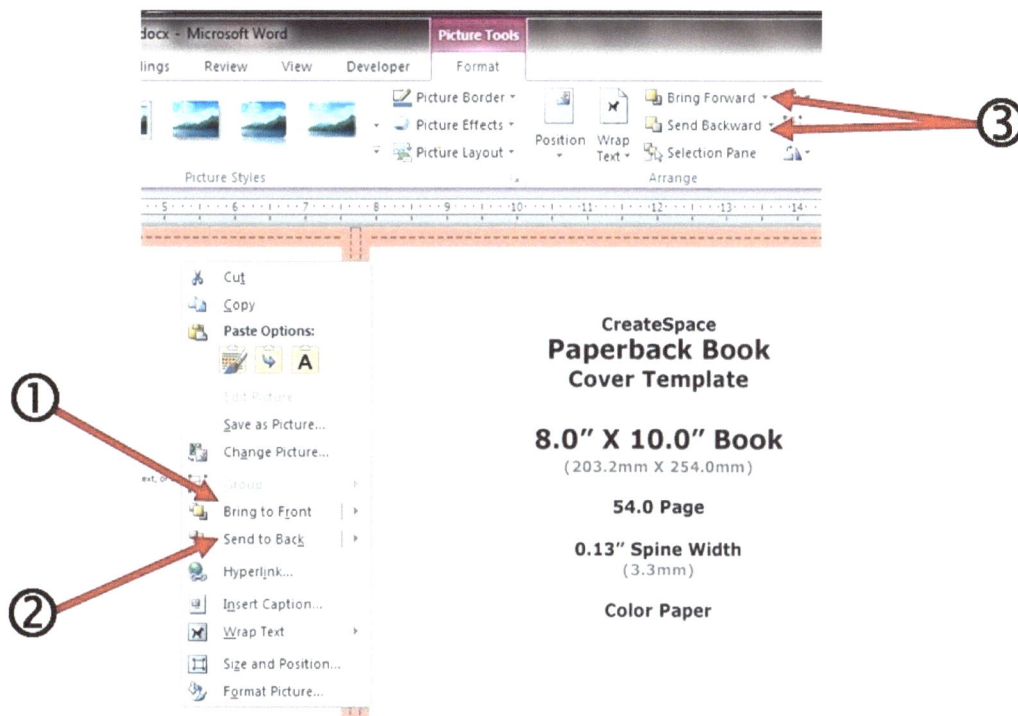

Figure 45. CS—Ordering - Bring to Front / Send to Back

1. In the Cover document, click anywhere in the working area.
2. Insert the design file (the artwork in JPG format) by <**Insert**><**Picture**>.
3. With the image still selected, click on <**Wrap Text**> <**In Front of Text**> to float the image. Note that the new image won't be visible until this step is performed. Initially, it will be just the outline.
4. If the new image *disappears*:
   a. Click <**ESC**> and then click on the template image (rectangle with pink frame).
   b. Drag the template image down and/or to the side until the design image appears.
   c. Apply the <**Wrap Text**><**In Front of Text**> to the design image.
   d. Move the template image back to the correct position, right click on it and select <**Send to Back**>. The new image should appear to sit on top of the template image.
5. Stretch and drag the new image to completely cover the document work area. No pink frame should show.

Note: The proceeding steps assume that the cover design is one file. If there are separate images for the front, spine and/or back, use the same technique, but position the various images in the correct juxtaposition so that no underlying colors are visible.

4.4. Adding Text

Look at the design image and think about what text you want to include on the book cover and where it will be positioned. The color of the text is also important. Black font on a dark background may not show up; white or yellow might be a better choice. To get ideas on how the verbiage is integrated, look at books that appeal to you and consider what's on them. The following elements should be included, unless they are incorporated into the design image:

- Front
  - Title
  - Subtitle (if necessary)
  - Author's name
- Spine
  - Title
  - Author's name
- Back
  - Description
  - Author's picture
  - Author's biography
  - Website, blog, twitter handle or any other contact information
  - Credit to artist

Note: Amazon/CreateSpace uses the verbiage on your book cover to determine Author, Title and Subtitle. My original books were attributed to *E. Sabbag*; Amazon would not allow me to enter *Evelyn Sabbag* as an alias. Therefore, this book is by *Evelyn Sabbag* to allow this nom de plume. It's still non-trivial to link the two. Whenever possible, pick a name and stick with it.

The verbiage that appears on the cover is positioned in a shape called a <**Text Box**>. These *boxes* can be manipulated just like an image, unlike standard text. When setting up the text inside the boxes, be careful when selecting the font as some fonts will not translate into a PDF. The best approach is to use default fonts even if you've found some really great fonts somewhere on the Internet.

1. Click on the design image in the area that the text will be placed.
2. Click on <**Insert**><**Shapes**> and then the **Text Box** icon under <**Basic Shapes**> (**Figure 46-1**). Note that this icon will appear under <**Recently Used Shapes**> after it has been selected.

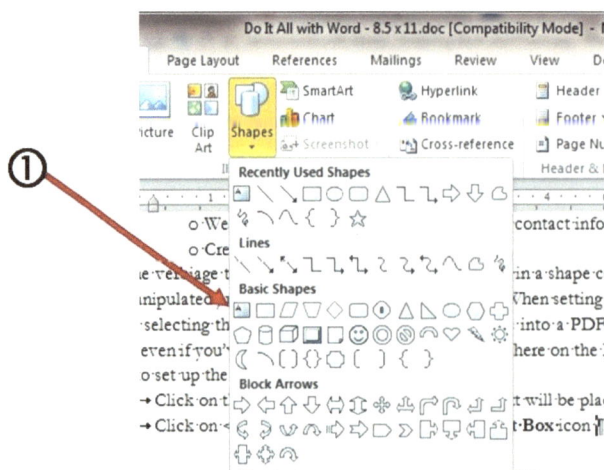

Figure 46. CS—Inserting a Text Box

3. A black cross will replace the cursor; this dictates the upper left corner of the text box. Click on the location of the text and continue to hold the left mouse key while dragging the cursor to create the text box. The resulting text box will resemble that in **Figure 47**.

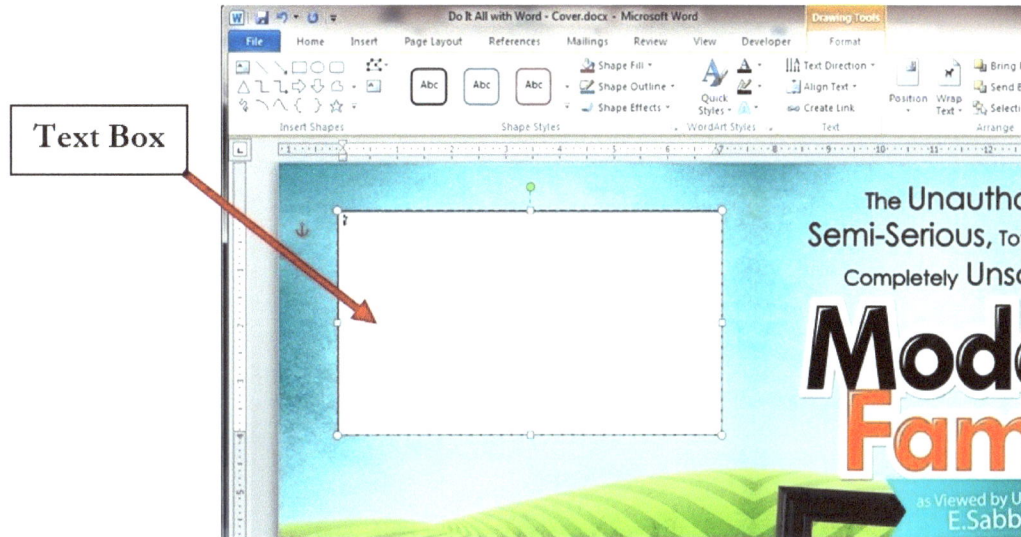

Figure 47. CS—Initial Text Box Insertion

4. Click inside the text box and type in the desired verbiage.
5. Once the text is complete, type **<CTRL><A>**. This selects all the text.
6. Click on **<Home>** and select the desired font attributes such as the font face, size, alignment, bold, italics, underline, etc. (**Figure 48**). Leave the color at the default setting for now.

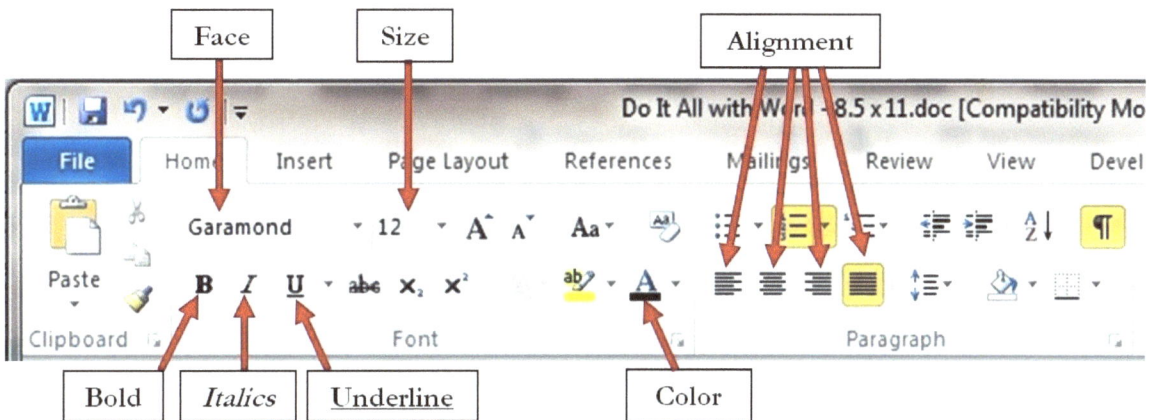

Figure 48. CS—Font Attributes

7. Before continuing with formatting the text box, check for fit and placement. Select the design image and then right click. Select **<Send to the Back>** from the drop down menu and see where the text lines up with the template. Ensure the text box doesn't overlap any of the pink areas or the yellow bar code space.(**Figure 49**)

Note: The font is set at the default color, black, when checking for fit because lighter colors, especially white, will *disappear* into the template image. Once the fit is verified and the design image moved back to the front, the text within the box can be set to the correct color (**Figure 48**).

8. Repeat steps 1-7 for each separate text area. Note that it's easier to place the text with separate text boxes than trying to make one text box and applying different styles to different areas.

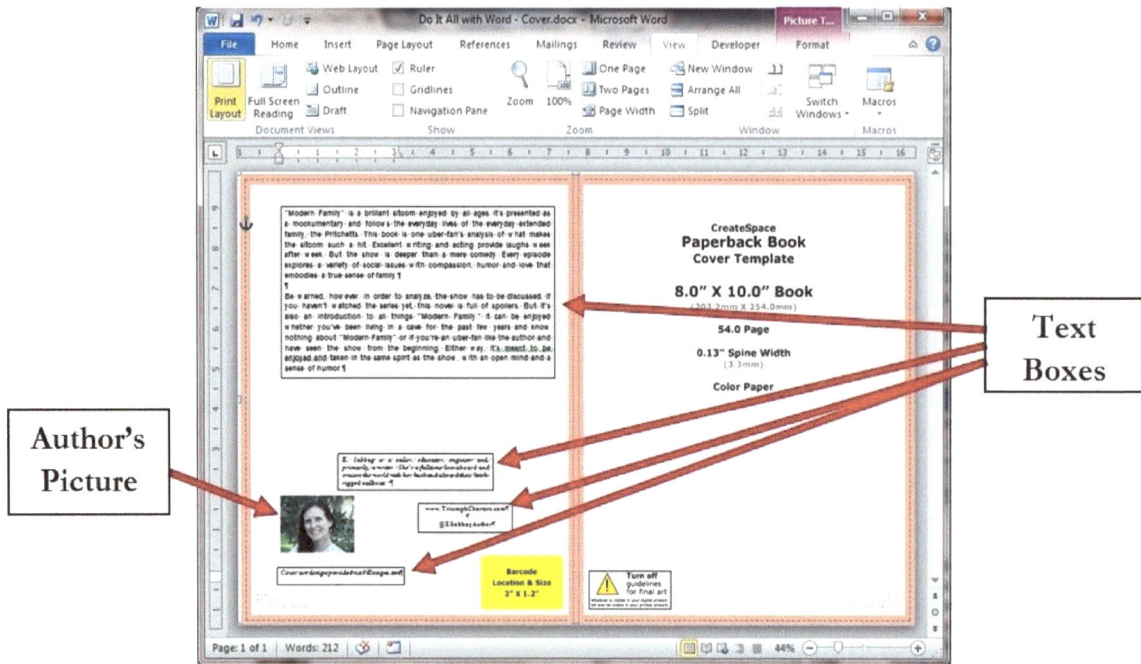

Figure 49. CS—Text Box Fit and Placement

9. After ensuring the text boxes are placed correctly, click anywhere in the template image, right click and select <**Send to the Back**> from the drop down menu. The cover now resembles **Figure 50**.

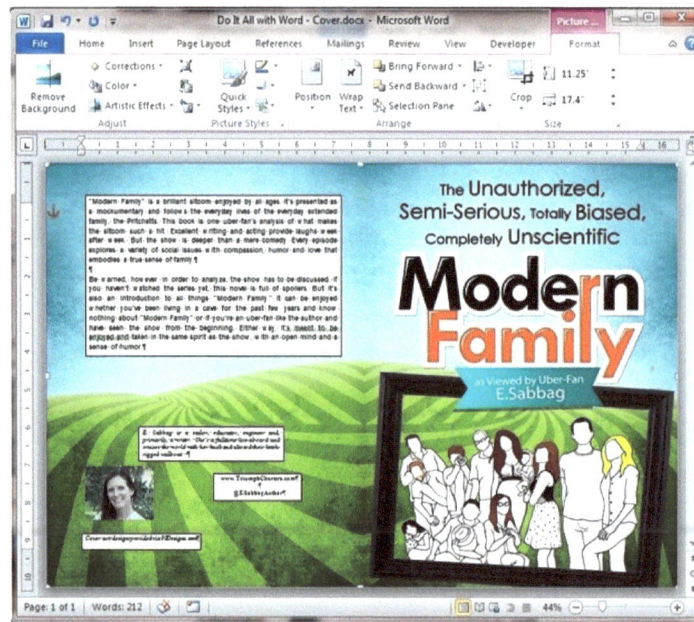

Figure 50. CS—Text Box Fit and Placement - Design Image on Top

10. Right click on the outline of each text box. Select <**Format Shape**> from the drop down menu. In the <**Format Shape**> dialogue box (**Figure 51**) select:

    a.   <**Fill**> - No Fill

    b.   <**Line Color**> - No Line

Note: If any of the text is copied from either the web or another application, it may contain hidden formatting direction that cannot be removed by Word®. If you run into anything weird, copy the text into a text editor such as Notepad, then copy it back into Word®.

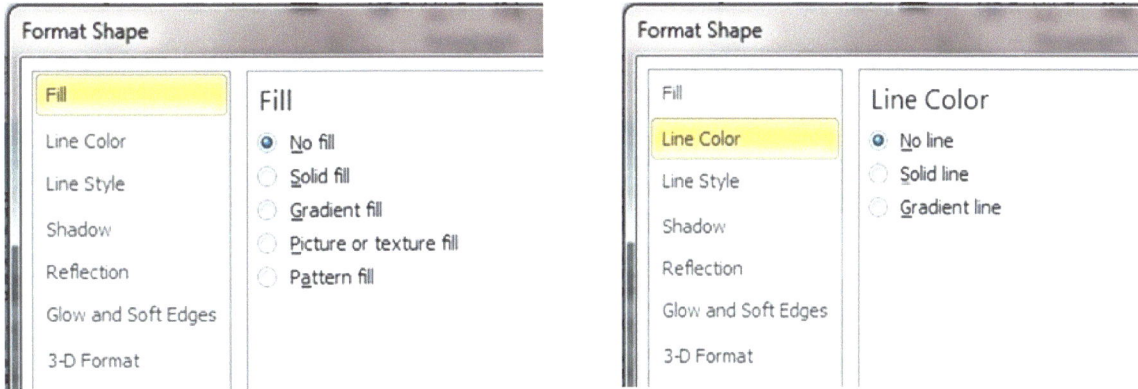

Figure 51. CS—Format Shape Dialogue Box

11. When finished, the cover document should resemble **Figure 52**.

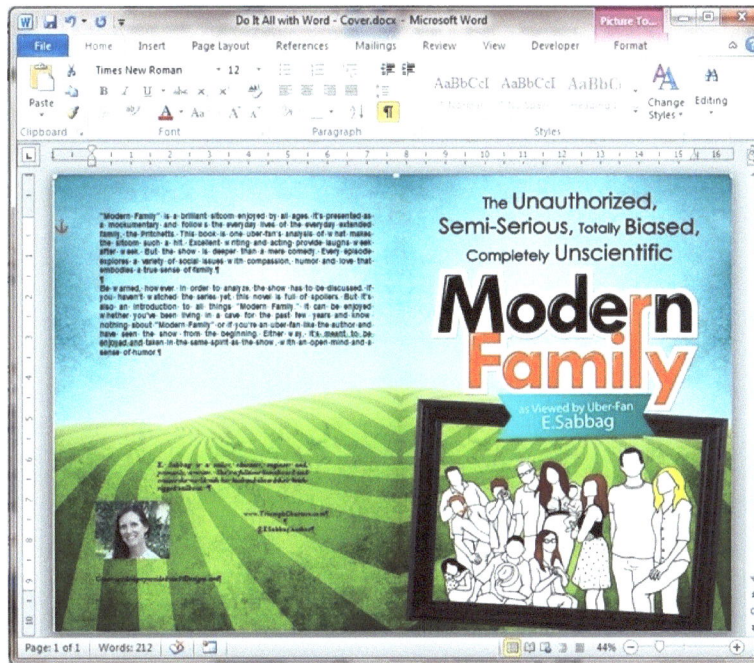

Figure 52. CS—Cover Art with Verbiage (Text Boxes)

Notice that the sample cover art does not have verbiage on the spine, such as Title and Author. This is because the book is too narrow to accommodate this. If you want to add text to the spine, add a text box similar to the other boxes, but right click on the frame of the text and navigate to the <**Text Box Tools**> tab on the toolbar. Click on the <**Rotate**> icon on the right and rotate the text box 90° clockwise. Position the resulting text box into place on the spine.

Note: For the rotate option to work, <**Compatibility Mode**> must be removed by saving the file in the newest format.

If you're satisfied with the cover, save the docx / doc file and then save the file as a PDF. If the PDF looks okay, move on to **Chapter 5 CS—Submission**. If not, modify as necessary and save again.

Chapter 5.CS—Submission

5.1. ISBN

The time has come to bite the bullet and select an ISBN choice. This must be included in the interior PDF.

If you want to retain full control of your book and be able to sell it through any retailer outlet, obtain an ISBN (or block of ISBN's for a cost savings) from Bowker Identification services on their website at https://www.myidentifiers.com. This is my choice for ISBN; the imprint (publisher name) is *Triumph Ventures, Inc.*, which is the corporation I run along with my husband.

If you only have one book and/or only want to distribute through Amazon and its associated channels, select the free ISBN from CreateSpace. Note that once this selection is chosen and the progress saved, it cannot be changed. Also, once the book is released for publication, this value cannot be changed.

Regardless of which ISBN route you choose, navigate to the ISBN section of your CreateSpace project (**Section 2.6.2**) and fill out the ISBN information. Then copy the numbers and insert them into the manuscript in the beginning of the book. Ensure the formatting matches the rest of the page manually or with the <**Format Painter**> (the little paint brush on the <**Home**> toolbar. Once the ISBN has been copied into the manuscript, save the document as a PDF in preparation for submission.

5.2. Interior / Cover PDF's

With the PDF's completed for the interior and cover art, it's time to return to CreateSpace and submit the files for review. Log into CreateSpace, click on the appropriate project and click on <**Interior**> under <**Setup**>(**Figure 6-4**) . The section in **Figure 53** will appear.

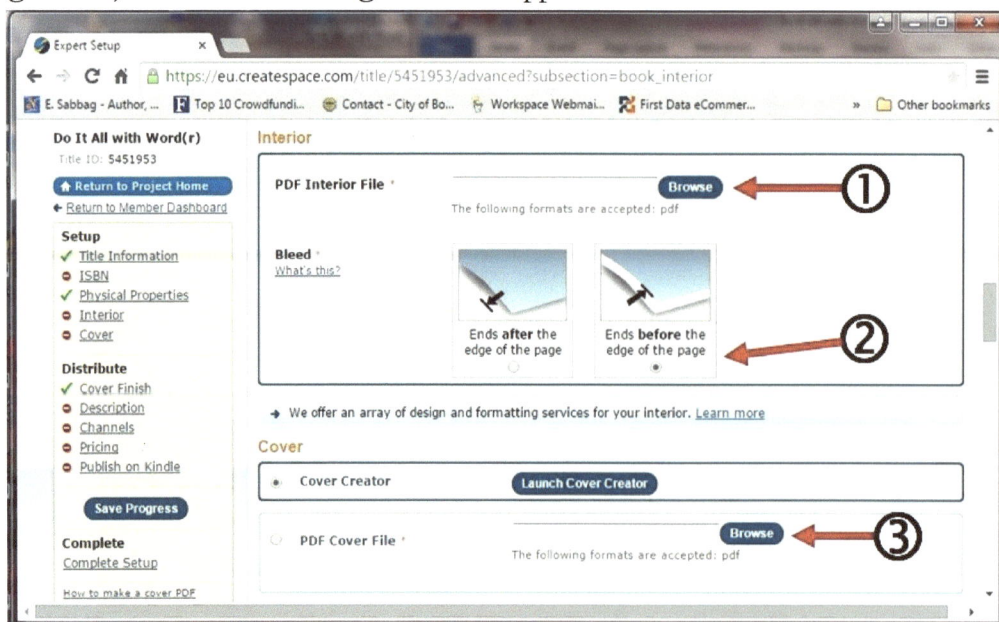

Figure 53. CS—Submitting Interior and Cover PDF's

Click on <**Browse**> to upload both the <**PDF Interior File**>(**Figure 53-1**) and <**PDF Cover File**>(**Figure 53-3**).

The <**Bleed**> (**Figure 53-2**) under <**Interior**> refers to the bleed margins. If the book is a graphics intensive book where the images go all the way to the edge of the page, with no white/cream around the edges, select the first bullet <**Ends *after* the edge of the page**>. If it's a book with no images or standard images (such as this one), select the second bullet <**Ends *before* the edge of the page**> (default).

5.3. Distribution Information / Submit for Review

You may have noticed as you're working within the CreateSpace project that there are a list of errors and issues at the bottom of the page. These are useful as a check list and, while they must be cleared up before publication is possible, they will disappear as you work through each section.

Once the PDF's are uploaded, there is a block of information under the heading <**Distribute**> that must be filled in prior to submitting the files for review (**Figure 54**).

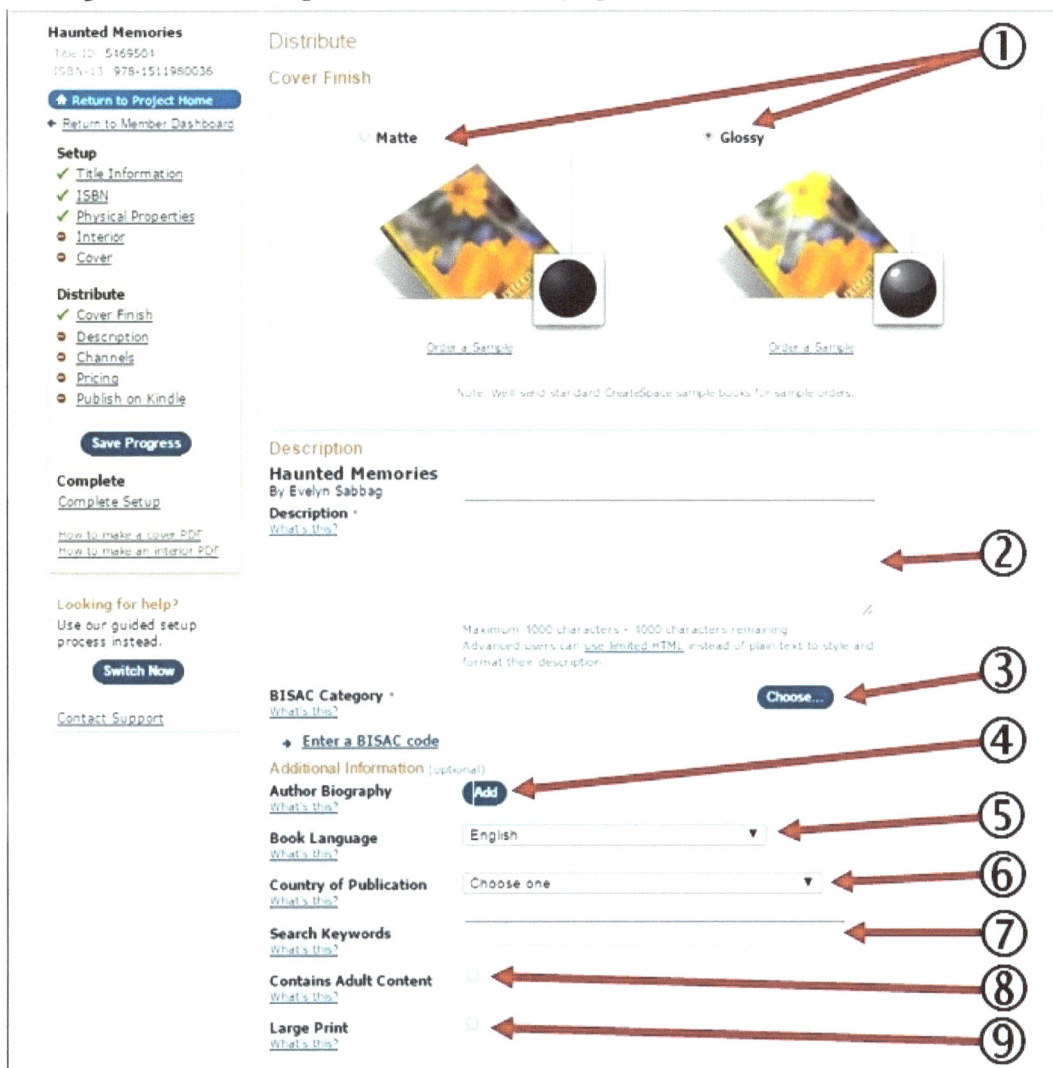

Figure 54. CS—Distribute Details

1 *Cover Finish—There are two choices, <**Matte**> and <**Glossy**>. I've used both and it depends on the atmosphere you want to convey. <**Glossy**> gives a crisp, bolder image that pops. It's good for colorful, graphic covers or ones with photos with a lot of detail. <**Matte**> has a soft, dreamy quality and is good for water-color like covers and romantic images. Once you order a print proof (and I highly recommend this—especially for your first project), you can see what it looks like and, if you don't like the result, order a second one with the other finish. It's not concrete until you approve the book for publication.

2 *Description —This paragraph has a maximum limit of 4000 characters. It is what will be used in Amazon and the various channels to present your book. It should convey the essence of the story, but not provide spoilers. I duplicate the verbiage on the back of the book—the blurb—in this paragraph.

Note that you are given the option to use limited HTML to put in paragraph breaks, italics and other basic HTML. If you click on **<use limited HTML>**, a pop-up menu will show you what HTML tags are available. Tags work as bracketing direction to a web page. *Italics* use the tag pair <i> </i>. There's always a letter or two for the first tag and a forward slash and the same letter(s) in the second tag. The dialogue goes in between. **<i> Haunted Memories</i>** will display on a webpage as ***Haunted Memories*** (no tags appear.). Internet searches on HTML will describe the options and give examples. If in doubt, consider plain text and make it work.

3 *BISAC Category—This field is how the book will be categorized on the distribution channels. The example project I've been using, *Haunted Memories*, is classified as **Fiction/Romance/Paranormal**. Be truthful in this categorization; bad reviews will come if you misrepresent your book, no matter how well meaning.

4 *Author Biography* (Optional)—I highly recommend you set up an author's page on Amazon. Even if you only have one book, people like to know about the authors. Duplicate that biography if you don't want to keep writing a new one. Or leave it blank and let the author's page be your information.

5 *Book Language—Default is **<English>**, select whatever is appropriate for your book.

6 *Country of Publication—**<United States>** is at the top of the drop down list, but choose the appropriate one for your project.

7 *Search Keywords* (Optional)—While **<Search keywords>** are optional, they are highly recommended. This is what the search engines such as Google use when a browser initiates a search. Not only is it important to input meaningful and relevant keywords, if you misrepresent your work it may be blackballed by Amazon, Google and others. An example would be to put in 'J.K. Rawlings' for your Young Adult fantasy novel. If you are J. K. Rawlings and you're reading my book because you want to self-publish, I'm honored… Up to five keywords are allowed and they can be phrases, separated by commas. Make sure and put your own name. Silly, I know, but critically important. Examples for *Haunted Memories* are "Paranormal Romance, Rural Ohio, Woman Empowerment, E. Sabbag, Evelyn Sabbag".

8 *Contains Adult Content* (Optional)—Self-explanatory – you make the decision.

9 *Large print* (Optional)—If the font in your book is 16 point or higher, it can be listed as **<Large Print>**. It will also be listed in the other categories as applicable; this is an additional attribute. Note, this does not apply to children's books.

Once these fields are completed, click on **<Submit for Review>**. The disclaimer is that it can take up to 24 hours for the review, but most of my books are reviewed within a few hours. This review checks the files for print *readiness,* but does not comment on content or marketability. Any issues are flagged and reported. Once the review returns with no issues or, issues that were corrected by CreateSpace, a proof can be examined. While waiting for the review to complete, **<Channels>** and **<Pricing>** can be addressed.

5.4. Channels

Once the <**Interior**> PDF is uploaded and the <**Distribute**> details are filled in, the distribution channels shown in **Figure 55** can be selected. If you have a CreateSpace ISBN, all channels are available. If you provided the ISBN, <**Libraries & Academic Institutions**> are excluded. Note that these institutions can still obtain your book, it just won't be automatically provided through Amazon / CreateSpace.

Click on <**Select**> for each channel. In the words of the late, great John Belushi in *Animal House*, "…it don't cost nuttin'…" Having badly paraphrased a cool actor, <**Expanded Distribution**> channels have a different impact on list price than <**Standard Distribution**> channels. This will be discussed in section **5.5 Pricing**.

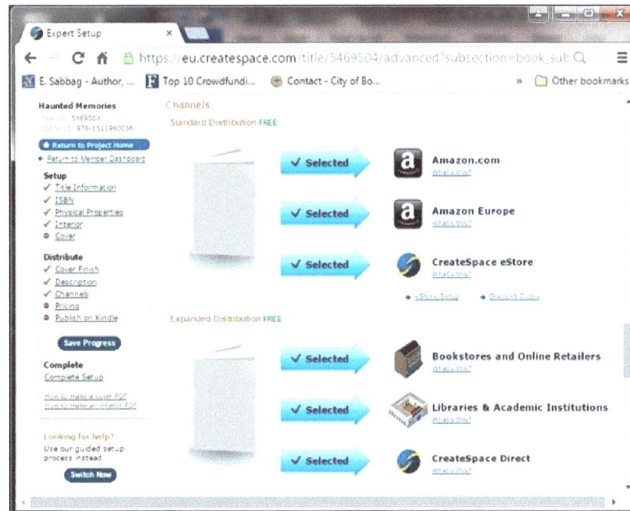

Figure 55. CS—Distribution Channels

5.5. Pricing

The pricing section acts as a calculator that shows what royalties will be paid out for each channel. A minimum list price is given, based on your book size, and it will produce reasonable royalties, but may provide a $0 royalty for certain channels (**Figure 56**). If the price required for > 0 royalty is too high and you don't want to give the book away, you can remove the <**Expanded Distribution**> channels.

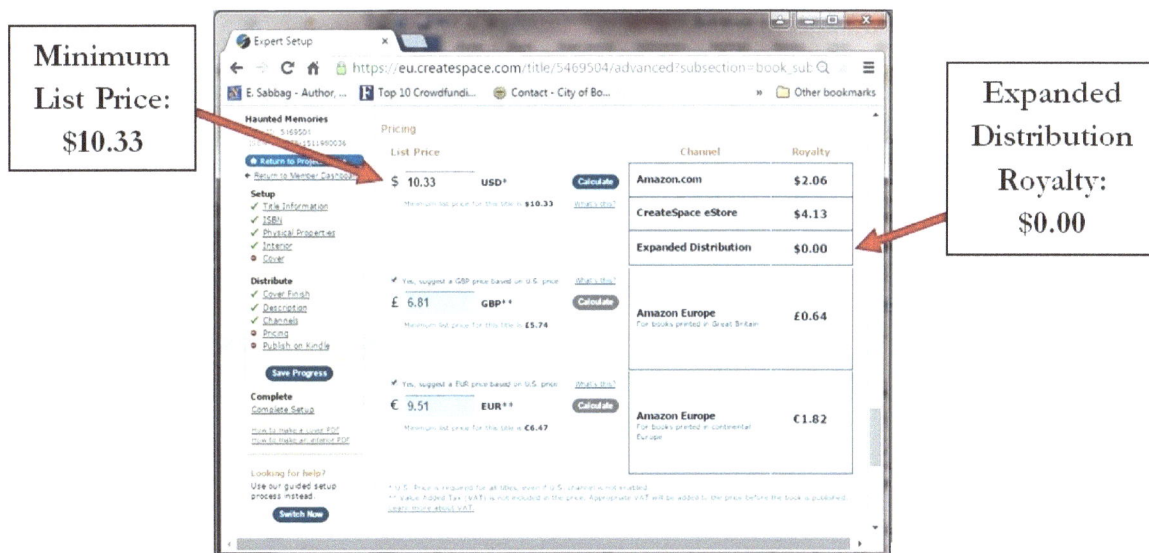

Figure 56. CS—Pricing

5.6. Review and Proof

Once the files are uploaded and the information is completely filled in, the warnings at the bottom of the Project Homepage should disappear. A message indicating it is time to submit should take their place (**Figure 57**)

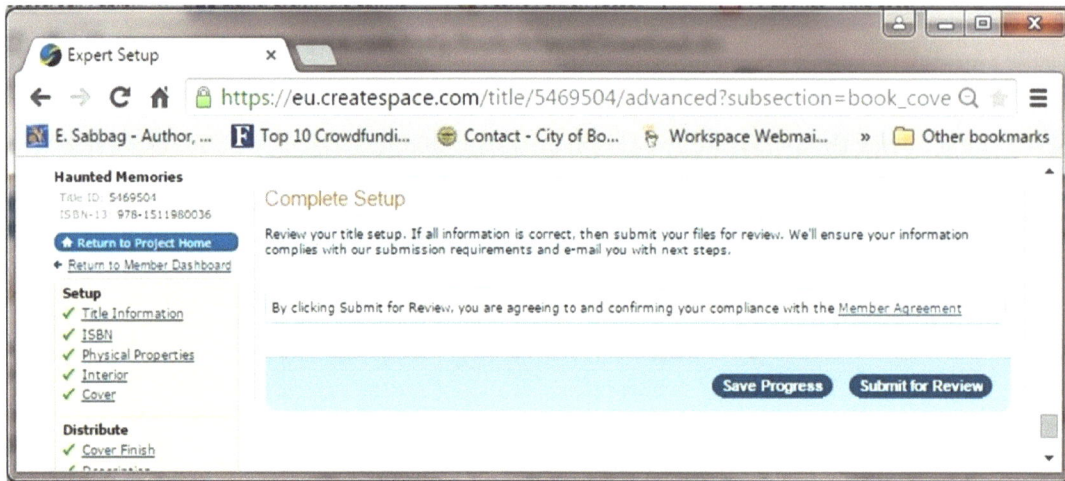

Figure 57. CS—Complete Setup

Click on <**Submit for Review**> and wait for a response. As mentioned earlier, the pop-up window says the files will be checked within 24 hours and the results will be emailed at that time, but mine have always come in much faster.

The review for the example project, *Haunted Memories*, revealed one issue and two warnings (**Figure 58**).

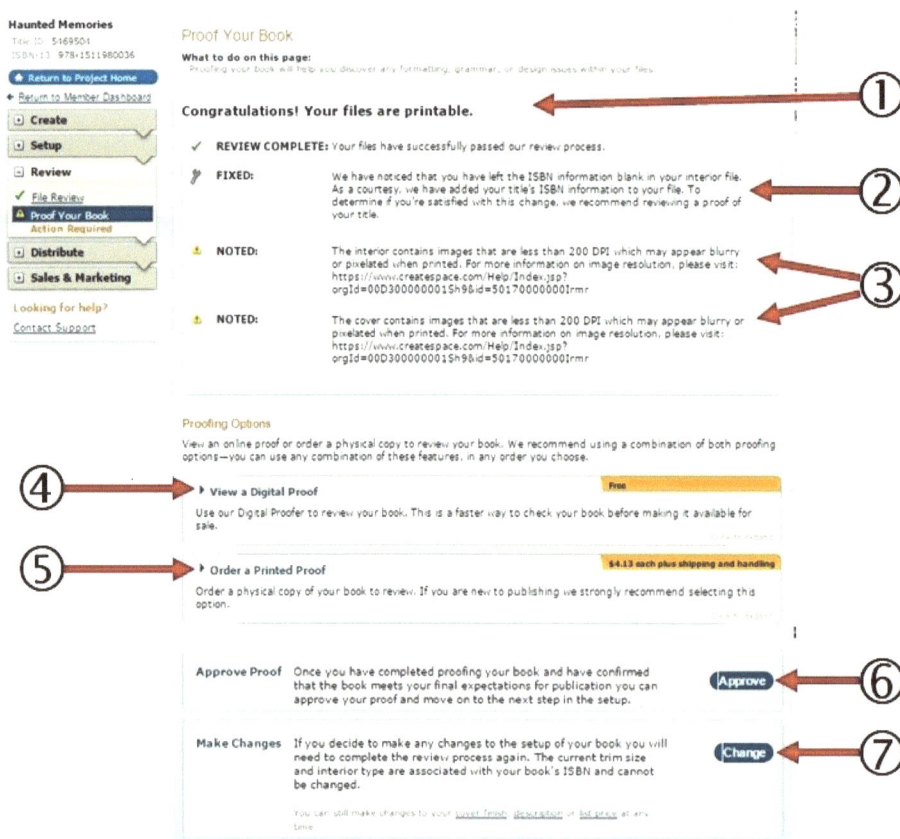

Figure 58. CS—Review Results

1 **Congratulations! Your files are printable**—At this point, you could approve the book and you're published. But, especially if this is the first pass, DON'T DO IT! Having a *printable* book does not necessarily equate to a *quality* book. Since you already have so much time and energy invested, be patient and do a little more work. Note, if you've diligently followed the instructions in this workbook, there's no reason to believe your book won't pass the first review.

2 **Fixed** —*"We have noticed that you have left the ISBN information blank in your interior file. As a courtesy, we have added your title's ISBN information to your file. To determine if you're satisfied with this change, we recommend reviewing a proof of your title."* Oops… I do this periodically. Luckily, CreateSpace puts in the ISBN, but I'm rarely satisfied with the format. Time for a <**Digital Proof**>.

3 **Notice**—Images somewhere in the file do not meet the minimum resolution and may be fuzzy and/or pixelated. This can be analyzed with first the <**Digital Proof**> and then the <**Print Proof**>.

4 **View a Digital Proof**—One of the best review tools around. Details will be covered in section **5.6.1**.

5 **Order a Printed Proof**—Once you've reviewed the <**Digital Proof**> and made changes, if necessary, ORDER A PRINT PROOF! Sorry for yelling, but I can't emphasize this enough.

6 **Approve Proof**—This is the point of no return for various details—everything except for **Chapter 5,** sections **5.2-5.5**. Do not click this option until you're absolutely sure the book is ready for publication.

7 **Make Changes**—This is one of the places in the CreateSpace project interface that I would make a change. Ironic, huh? This selection should be placed BEFORE the point of no return <**Approve Proof**>. Making changes results in another <**Review**>, which can take up to 24 hours, but it's well worth it. Years from now when you're looking back on your very successful first book, the extra 6-24 hours will be meaningless.

5.6.1. Digital Proof
Click on <**Digital Proof**> (**Figure 58-4**) to expand the selection in **Figure 59.**

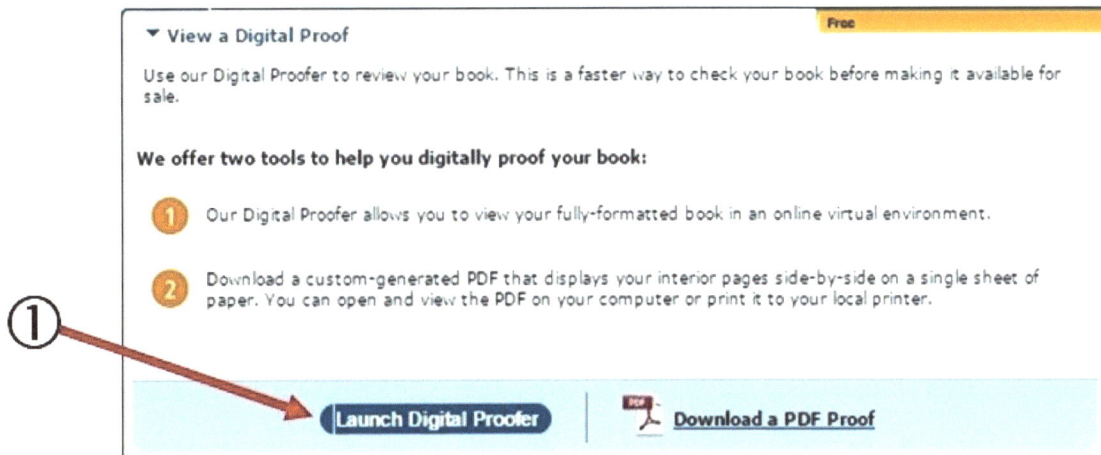

Figure 59. CS—View a Digital Proof

There are two options when viewing a <**Digital Proof**>. Nothing keeps you from using both, but I find the <**Digital Proofer**> the most useful. Click on <**Launch Digital Proofer**> (**Figure 59-1**) to view a web-based version of your book. There, you can focus on the issues and determine if they require modification.

Recall that I had forgotten to insert the ISBN into my PDF. Checking that page with the <**Digital Proofer**> reveals that the alignment is incorrect(**Figure 60**). I will have to make a change (**Figure 58-1**) and resubmit the interior PDF. Hey, I'm detail-obsessed, but that's what makes a quality book!

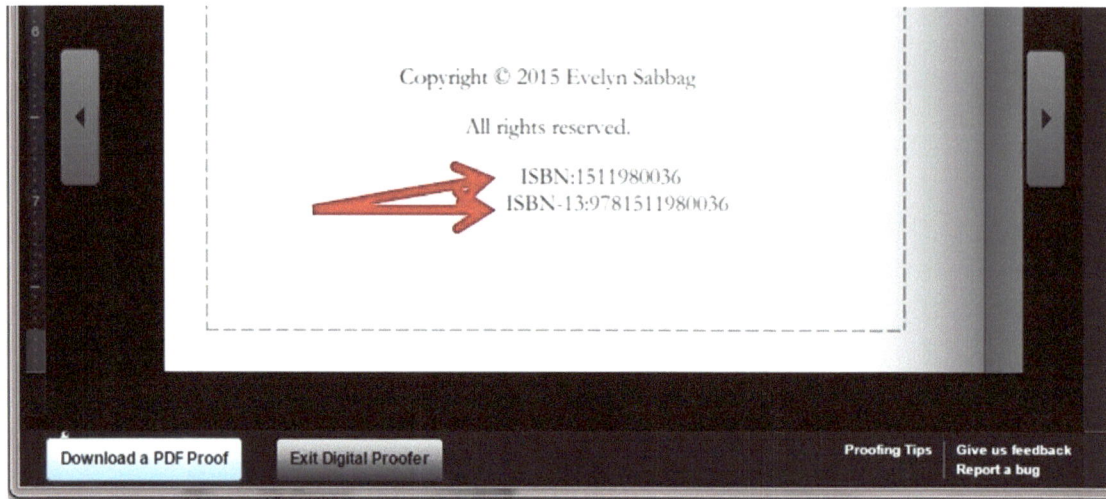

Figure 60. CS—CreateSpace ISBN Insertion

The <**Notice**>s refer to the image quality. This project has no pictures or embedded images, which implies it's referring to the text quality. That looks okay, so it can be ignored. If there are images in your file, navigate to <**File**><**Options**><**Advanced**>, scroll down to <**Image Size and Quality**> and click on the box beside <**Do not compress images in file**>. The file size may grow, but that's the trade-off you have to live with. If the <**Digital Proofer**> and/or <**PDF Proof** > look okay, order a <**Print Proof**> to examine the finished product. Trust me on this, it's worth it.

5.6.2. Print Proof

A week or more has passed and you've received the <**Print Proof**>, possibly made a few changes and resubmitted, and even ordered another or more rounds of <**Print Proof**>'s. Once you're satisfied with your project, it's time to publish. This is accomplished by clicking on <**Approve Proof**>(**Figure 58-6**).

CONGRATULATIONS! Your book is now published. After this momentous occasion, there are some details that can be modified (**Chapter 5,** sections **5.2-5.5**), but ensure the content isn't drastically changed or a new ISBN will have to be issued. This is also a good time to return to Bowker®, if you purchased an ISBN, and complete the information on that site. This is where external agencies obtain shipping and content details, so it's critically important that it reflect reality.

Once this phase is complete, CreateSpace offers the ability to submit your files to Kindle Digital Publishing (KDP) automatically. A conundrum is that the file uploaded to CreateSpace is a PDF, which doesn't translate well to eBooks. As a result, some information—title, description, contributors, category, and cover art—will be transferred, but not the interior file (click the option to upload this yourself) or subtitle. You will be asked about the Publishing Rights Status (section **6.4 Publishing Rights, Target Audience, Release Option**) and to select the Digital Rights Management (DRM) option (section **6.6.4 Uploading for Review**). These can be changed up to publication, so just pick one for now and proceed to **Chapter 6 Kindle Digital Publishing (KDP)—New Project** to convert your manuscript to an eBook.

Chapter 6. Kindle Digital Publishing (KDP)—New Project

6.1. Introduction to eBooks

"I though this was supposed to be easy!!" Grammatical mistake and all, this is a quote from the KDP user forum. The response was *"It's not easy, and those who think it is are probably not formatting very well."* This is the introduction to eBook formatting because it sums it up perfectly. eBooks are easier than formatting for POD books, but that's a relative concept. Both are challenging and require attention to detail, persistence and a LOT of patience. Follow the steps, review any modification you make and you'll create a quality eBook. KDP is the eBook publisher for Amazon and the two connect seamlessly.

6.2. Log In to Existing Account

Access your account by navigating to https://kdp.amazon.com/. Sign in with your Amazon account if you have one (**Figure 61-1**) or create one and then sign in if you don't (**Figure 61-2**).

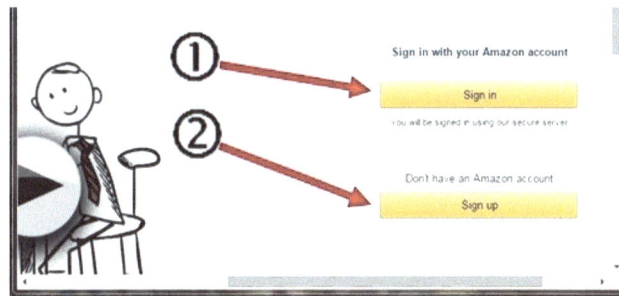

Figure 61. KDP Website—Log In to Amazon Account

Once logged in, a <**Bookshelf**> will appear with the <**Create New Title**> as the first choice if you didn't already set up the project via CreateSpace. Click on the blue cross(**Figure 62-1**) if this is a new project or proceed with the project setup if CreateSpace set it up for you.

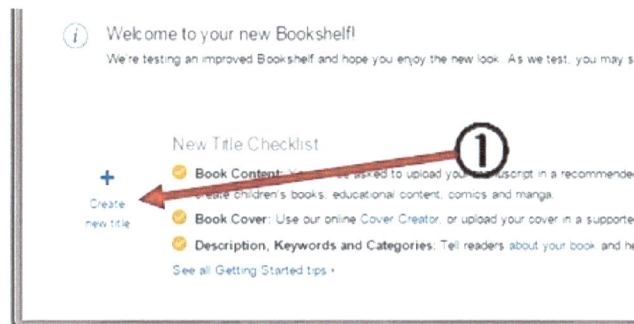

Figure 62. KDP—Create New Title

The next page will prominently display the opportunity to enroll in <**Kindle Select**> (**Figure 63**). This is a program available to Amazon customers. If your book is enrolled in this program and an Amazon customer (enrolled in <**Kindle Select**>) chooses to read your book, you will receive a portion of the cash fund dedicated to this program. For this privilege, you agree to not make your eBook available for sale anywhere other than Amazon for 90 days. If you're not planning on distributing your eBook through any other channel, it doesn't hurt to enroll. If you want to market it through Lulu or Barnes & Noble or even your own online store, pass on the opportunity. At the time of publication of this book, I have four self-published books that have solid sales. I have received less than a dollar from the Kindle Select Global Fund. For now, I'd leave it unchecked and move on to creating your eBook. Your choice.

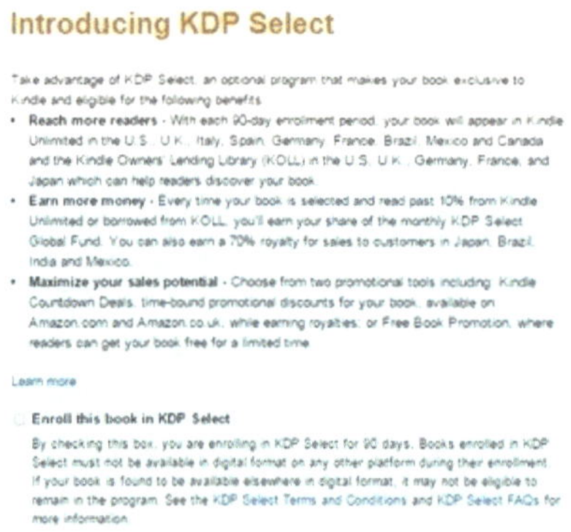

Figure 63. KDP—Enroll in Kindle Select

6.3. Book Details

The first section contains the <**Book Details**>. If you have a POD book already setup, duplicate all but the ISBN to allow your readers to seamlessly connect the two media.

Figure 64. KDP—Book Details

1. ***Book Name**—Fill in the name of the book exactly as it will be displayed on the eBook. It will be

used for search engines and indexing and should duplicate that of a POD, if one exists.

2. *Subtitle* (Optional)—This verbiage will be concatenated onto the title and will appear as *Title: Subtitle*. Note that the colon is added by the distributing entity.

3. *This book is part of a series* (Optional)—Click this check box if the book is in a series. Once you click it, the option to fill in the <**Series Title**> and <**Volume #**> will appear. Both of these fields are hidden until the check box is clicked.

4. *Edition Number* (Optional)—Fill in if appropriate. Otherwise, leave it blank.

5. *Publisher* (Optional)—If you have a publisher's name (imprint) and an ISBN, fill this in.

6. ***Description**—Enter the book's description, which will be used in catalogues. If there's a POD book, duplicate the description for consistency.

7. ***Book Contributors**—Click on <**Add contributors**> and select all contributory functions. As a minimum, the primary author must be added. This is the name or pseudonym of the author exactly as it should be displayed in the distribution catalogue.

8. ***Language**—Defaults to English. Use the drop down menu to select the appropriate language.

9. *ISBN* (Optional)—eBooks don't require ISBN's, but Libraries, online retailers and other entities are offering eBooks. An ISBN is useful for categorizing the work, making it visible and providing some copyright protection. KDP does not supply ISBN's – they must be obtained from an external provider such as Bowker® (https://www.myidentifiers.com/).

6.4. Publishing Rights, Target Audience, Release Option

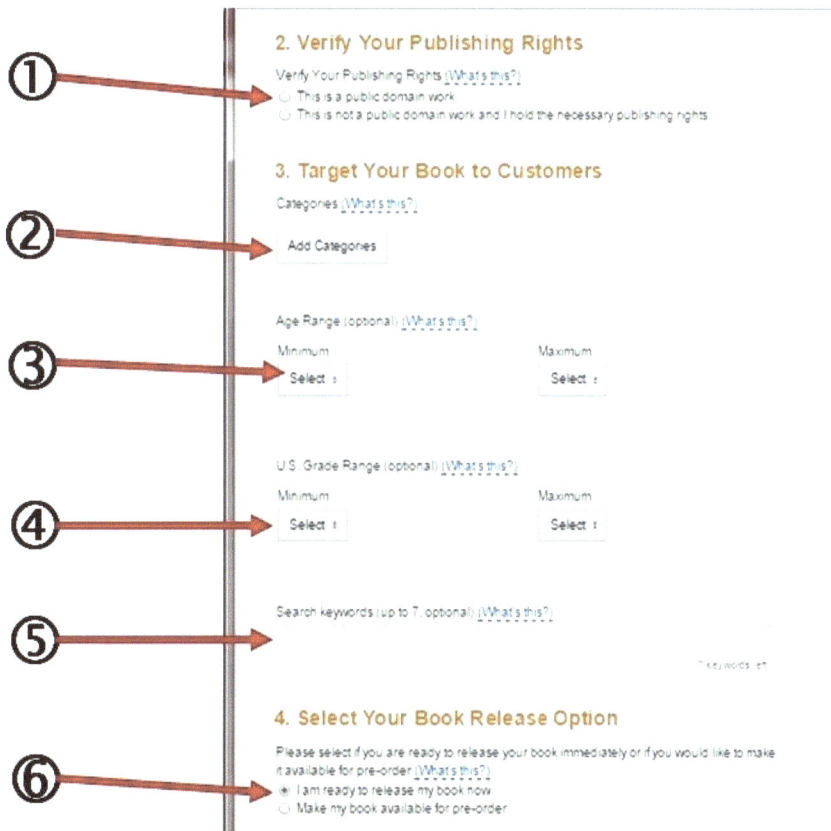

Figure 65. KDP—Publishing Rights, Target Audience and Release Options

1. ***Verify your Publishing Rights**—There are two choices, < **This is a public domain work** > and <**This is not a public domain work and I hold the necessary publishing rights**>. If the work

is completely yours, select <**…not a public domain work..**>. This would be a novel, How-to, etc. If it is public domain, make sure you hold the rights to publish it. Note that a public domain work is not eligible for the 70% royalty.

2. ***Add Categories**— This field is how the book will be categorized on the distribution channels. The example project I've been using, *Haunted Memories*, is classified as **Fiction/Romance/Paranormal**. Be truthful in this categorization; bad reviews will come if you misrepresent your book, no matter how well meaning. If there is a companion POD paperback, duplicate the category if possible.

3. *Age Range* (Optional)— This is most important for books targeted for children and young adults.

4. *U.S. Grade Range* (Optional)—Important for books that will be distributed to schools and/or libraries.

5. *Search Keywords* (Optional)—While <**Search keywords**> are optional, they are highly recommended. This is what search engines such as Google use when a browser initiates a search. Not only is it important to input meaningful and relevant keywords, if you misrepresent your work it may be blackballed by Amazon, Google and others. An example would be to put in 'J.K. Rawlings' for your Young Adult fantasy novel. If you are J. K. Rawlings and you're reading my book because you want to self-publish, I'm honored… Up to seven keywords are allowed and they can be phrases separated by commas. Make sure and put your own name. Silly, but critically important. Examples for *Haunted Memories* are "Paranormal, Romance, Ghost, Ohio, E. Sabbag, Evelyn Sabbag".

6. ***Select Your Book Release Option**— The book can be released now (first check bullet) or available for pre-order. The latter is good if you have a specific release date and are building a marketing campaign for it. This is one way to create a buzz, especially if this is one in a series.

6.5. eBook Cover

Creating a book cover for an eBook sets your book apart from the cookie cutter images available from KDP. To begin, you must have a high resolution (300+ DPI) image that you own the rights to. Don't just surf the web and select a picture you like—it's unethical and may cost you money in the long run. Especially if your book becomes a best seller! You don't want anyone to steal your work—don't steal someone else's. Review section **4.1 Obtaining the Artwork** for a discussion on obtaining the artwork.

Note: Images for eBooks MUST be RGB not CMYK. CMYK is a print format, but RGB works for print as well.

For an eBook, the digital reader, whether it's an actual reader such as a Kindle or a browser or other device, will control the size of the image. As a result, the cover art is submitted as a rectangle following certain constraints, regardless of the book's content. The verbiage and the sizing can be accomplished in **Paint**.

6.5.1. Inserting Text

Open the high resolution image of the front cover in **Paint.** Click on the *A* (**Figure 66-1**)on the top toolbar and insert a <**Text Box**> by clicking the cursor in the desired position on the image. The options in **Figure 66** will appear. Select the font type (**Figure 66-2**), size (**Figure 66-3**), bold (**Figure 66-4**), italics (**Figure 66-5**), underline (**Figure 66-6**), transparency (**Figure 66-7**), and color (**Figure 66-8**) and drag the text box to the final position.

Note: Once the text is positioned and the next element is selected (such as another text box), the last text cannot be modified or moved. <**UNDO**> is the only action possible. As a result, it's a good idea to save frequently and restore the last good image. The good news is that these images should be simple enough to show up well as a thumbnail.

Figure 66. KDP—Inserting Text onto Cover Art

When satisfied with the cover, it should resemble **Figure 67**.

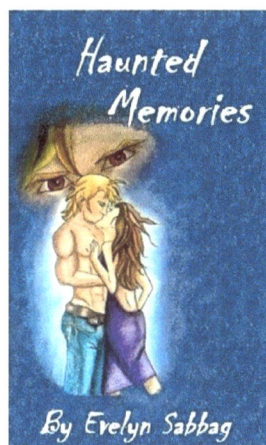

Figure 67. KDP—Sample Cover Art

6.5.2. Dimension and Format
KDP accepts images in JPG or TIFF format. I use only JPG, but the discussion applies equally to TIFF. Similar to a discussion on Ford and Chevy. Everyone has an opinion on which one is better, but, basically, they both get you where you need to go.

The dimensions (width and height) of the image has minimum and maximum requirements.

- **Ideal ratio**: At least a ratio of 1.6, width to height. That means the height is 1.6 times the width.
- **Minimum requirements**: Shortest side is 625 pixels; 1000 pixels on longest side
- **Recommended best quality**: 2500 on the longest side, which would mean the shortest side is 1562.

As a first try, work with the aspect ratio (width x height) of your image as it exists. This is to avoid distortion. Click on <**Resize**>(**Figure 68-1**), then select <**Pixels**> (**Figure 68-3**) when the dialogue box appears. Note that <**Maintain aspect ratio**> (**Figure 68-2**) is checked by default. Enter 2500 in the field entitled <**Vertical**>(**Figure 68-5**), click <**OK**> and see how the image looks. The <**Horizontal**> (**Figure**

68-4) must be at least 625 pixels and the overall file size must be less than 50 Mb.

Note: If the dimensions aren't working, try unchecking <**Maintain aspect ratio**> (**Figure 68-2**) and manipulating the sides independently.

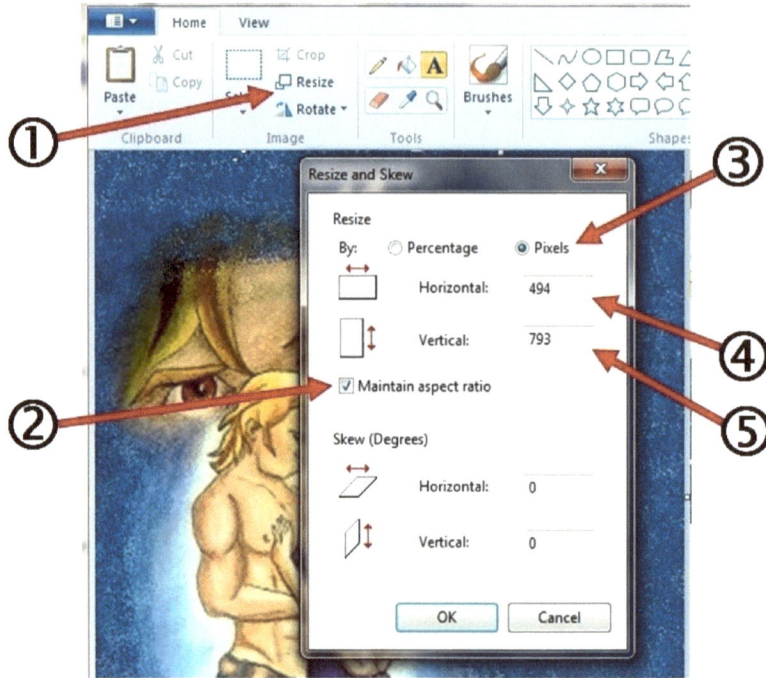

Figure 68. KDP—Cover Art Dimensions

When you're satisfied with how the image looks and you've met the minimum requirements (the 1.6 ratio is recommended, but not absolutely critical), save the image as a JPG (**Figure 69**).

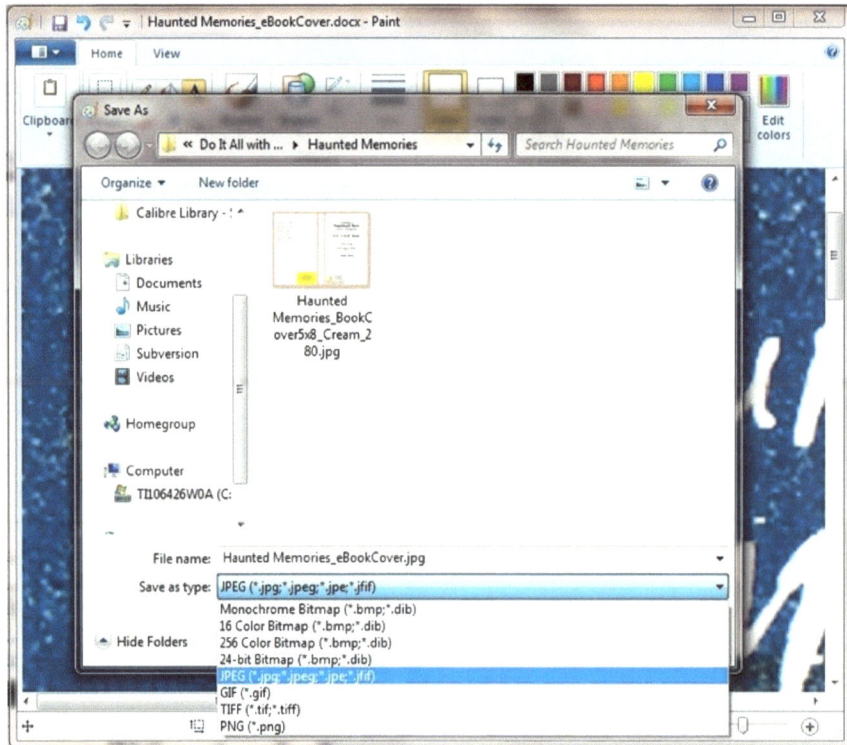

Figure 69. KDP—Save Cover Art as JPG

Note: For this image, when the <**Vertical**> side was set to 2500, the <**Horizontal**> side became 1557, which is extremely close to the perfect length, 1562. So it's good to go.

Once the file is saved, upload the image to KDP (**Figure 70-1**, **Figure 71**)

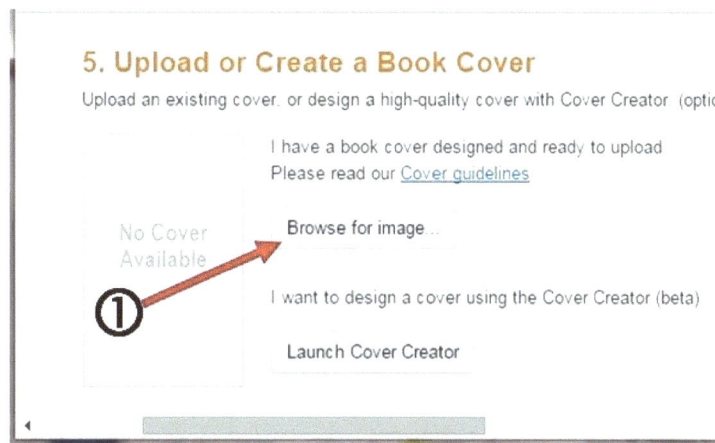

Figure 70. KDP—Upload a Book Cover

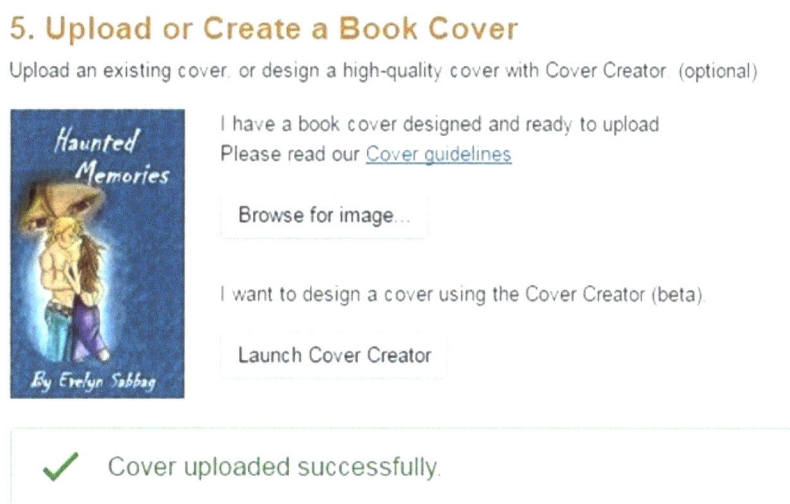

Figure 71. KDP—Uploaded eBook Cover

6.6. Interior Book File

Formatting doesn't have the same meaning in an eBook that it has in a print medium. An eBook Reader controls the document size, font size and margins. Therefore, any embedded formatting must be removed. To facilitate reformatting the manuscript, change the paper size to 17"x11" and apply this to the whole document (section **3.8 Changing Trim Size**) and zoom down to 57% or so. Save it to the eBook folder setup in section **2.3 PC Folder Structure, 1.b**. Also, make sure the formatting marks are visible (**Figure 16**). Once these are selected, review the section on formatting for a POD paperback, **Chapter 3 CS—Interior Formatting**, and make sure the following conventions are followed:

- Do not use tabs or extra spaces to center text or indent paragraphs. Use the indention feature (section **3.5.1 Paragraph Formatting**) or the <**Center**> feature (**Figure 27-1**). The preferred indentation for an eBook is 0.5", not 0.2" as preferred for print.

- Ensure all chapter titles are headings, not just bold and/or all caps (section **3.5.3 Chapter Headings**). Some conventions may have to be removed from your manuscript as they will not display properly in an eBook. They include:

- Extra blank line (hard return) after a paragraph will not display properly. Use the <**Paragraph**> <**Spacing**> <**After**> (**Figure 72-1**) feature to add extra spaces between paragraphs to indicate a change of scene.

Note: KDP recommends 10 pt after a paragraph. The up arrow increments/decrements in multiples of 6. 12 pt looks just as good and requires two clicks instead of typing in the characters every time.

Figure 72. KDP—Paragraph Formatting (Spacing) Dialogue Box

- Replace <**End of Section**> marks (**Figure 73-1**) with <**Page Break**>'s (**Figure 73-2**). The easiest way to do this is to place your cursor just before the <**End of Section**> and insert the <**Page Break**> by clicking on the icon. Then press <**DEL**> to remove the <**End of Section**>. Also remove any blank pages in this way. They do not have to be replaced with <**Page Break**>s.

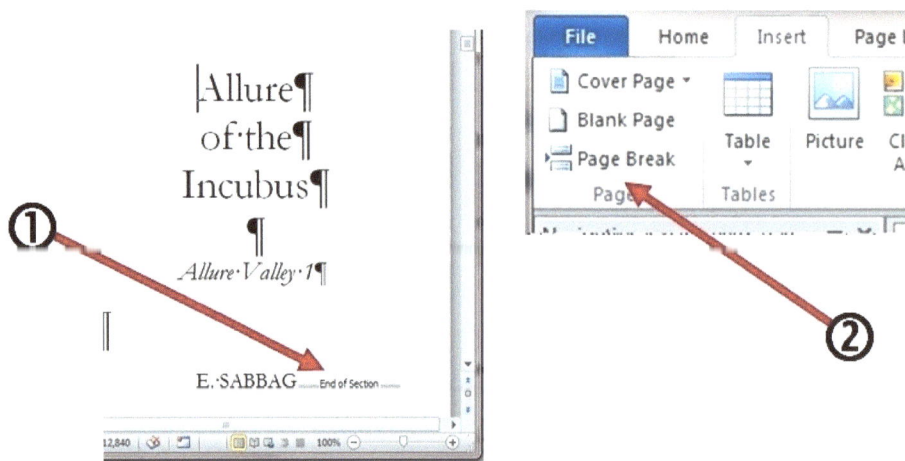

Figure 73. KDP—Replace Section Breaks with Page Breaks

- Remove all <**Header**> and <**Footer**> text. Refer to section **3.4 Headers**, but instead of typing in the information, delete it all. Repeat for the <**Footer**> and remove any page numbers or markings. If you delete all section breaks prior to this step, this will be easier.

- Windows default fonts can be used as well as bold, italics and underlining, but avoid custom fonts or special characters. Anything not understood by the converter will be replaced with '?'s. Note that standard Word® automatic bullets and numbering for lists should be okay. Always verify before publication.

6.6.1. Custom Style Pages (CSP)

If the manuscript used to create the eBook originated from a CreateSpace template, the custom styles (CSP) may cause issues with how the eBook displays. A common symptom is that the first paragraph in a chapter looks fine, but the next paragraph is a different sized font, different line spacing, random bold, etc. Make sure all text is either a <**Heading**> or <**Normal**>, not anything labeled CSP. To uncover CSP formatted areas, navigate to the <**Home**> tab on the toolbar and click on <**Find**> <**Advanced Find**> (**Figure 74**).

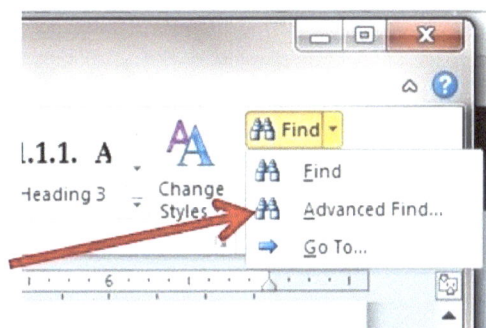

Figure 74. KDP—Advanced Find

On the pop-up dialogue box, click on < **More>>** > (if < **Less>>** > is not displayed) <**Format**> then <**Style**> and scroll down to the <**CSP…**> styles (**Figure 75**). Each incident of CSP formatting can be found by clicking on the results tab arrows on the search menu (**Navigation Pane**). Once found, change the paragraph/section to a standard Word® style such as <**Normal**>.

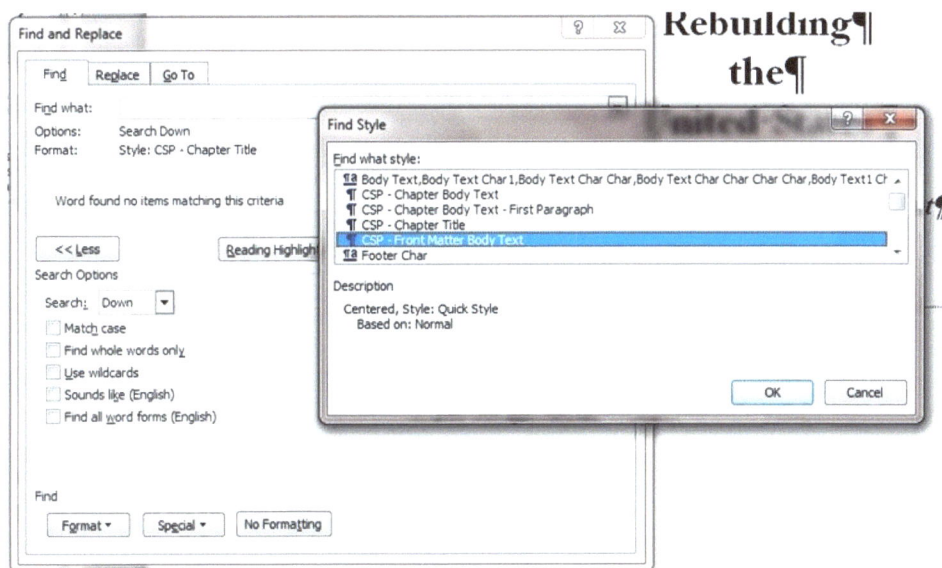

Figure 75. KDP—Advanced Find – Format Style CSP

Once all incidents of CSP formatting are removed, open the <**Styles**> dialogue box (**Figure 76-1**) and scroll to the CSP formats. Right click on each one and select <**Delete**> to remove the style (**Figure 76-2**).

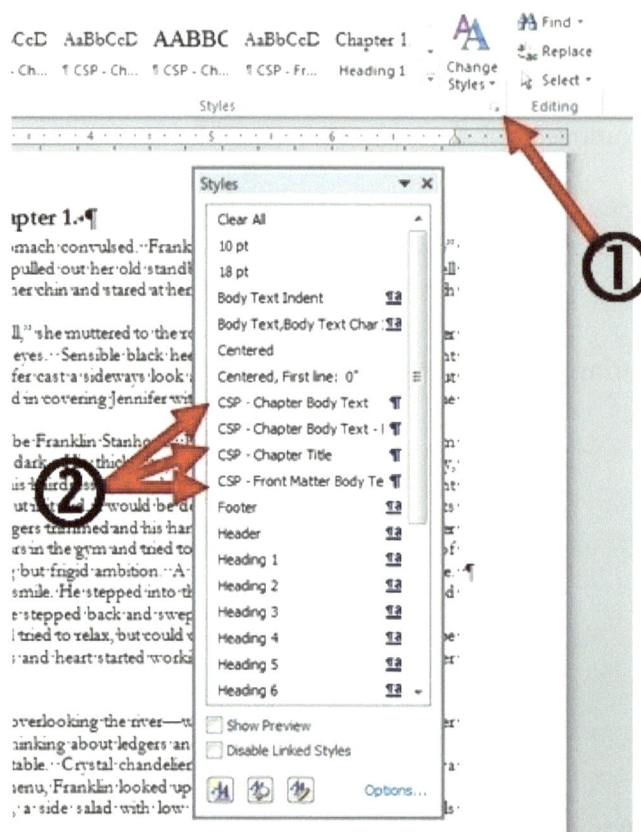

Figure 76. KDP—Remove CSP Formats from Styles

6.6.2. Graphics

eBooks, like traditional print books, require high quality images to translate well. Some readers, such as the original Kindles, are black and white only, whereas the newer devices can handle color. Be sure to check in both formats to ensure the images are legible.

Once the images are selected, are the correct resolution, and in a JPG format (see section **3.6.1 Preparing the Graphics Files** to verify and/or modify), insert them into the correct position using <**Insert**><**Picture**> (section **3.6.2 Inserting Graphics Files**). Do not *float* the image; leave it at the default <**Wrap Text**><**In line with text**> but center it by clicking on the center align icon (**Figure 27-1**).

Note: All graphics should be inserted this way. NEVER cut and paste from an external source as you don't have control over resolution, file type or hidden formatting .

6.6.3. Table of Contents and List of Figures

Navigate to <**References**> and click on the <**Table of Contents**> icon (**Figure 77**). Click on <**Insert Table of Contents**> at the bottom of the drop down menu. Set <**Show Levels**> to the desired amount of levels (the example is set to 1, but doesn't have to be) and unclick <**Show page numbers**>. In order for the lists to be actively linked to the appropriate headings in the document, the headings MUST be set up using the Word® <**Heading x**> selection (**3.5.3 Chapter Headings**).

Periodically and definitely before exiting the manuscript, make sure the TOC and the List of Figures (if one exists) are updated (section **3.7**).

Note: Page numbers have little meaning in an eBook. In addition to removing the page numbers, all references to them should be removed as well.

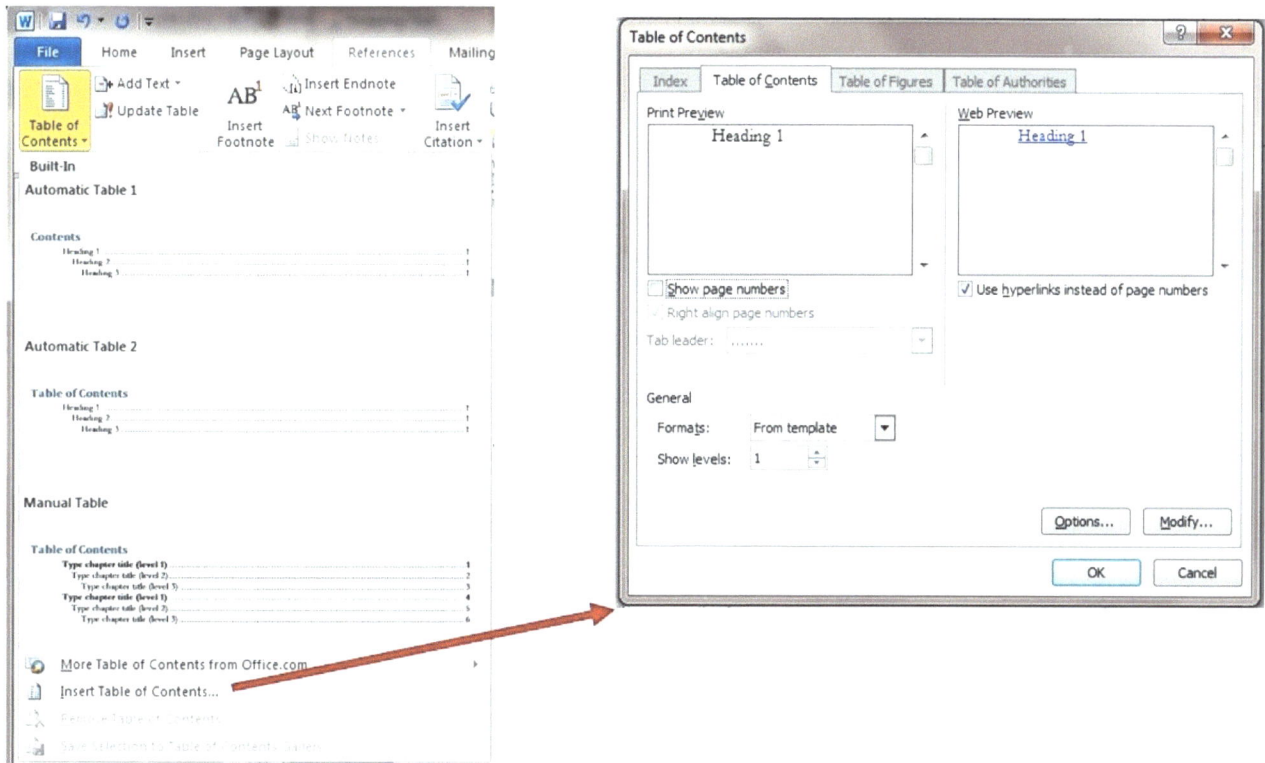

Figure 77. KDP—Insert Table of Contents

Once the TOC is inserted, navigate to the title and highlight the verbiage. With the text still selected, navigate to <**Insert**> <**Bookmark**> (**Figure 78**). When the <**Bookmark**> dialogue box appears, type in 'toc' and then <**Add**>. The dialogue box will close automatically. When the file is converted to an eBook format, it will pick up this bookmark.

Note: When you name the bookmarks, they cannot contain spaces or special characters, except for an underscore.

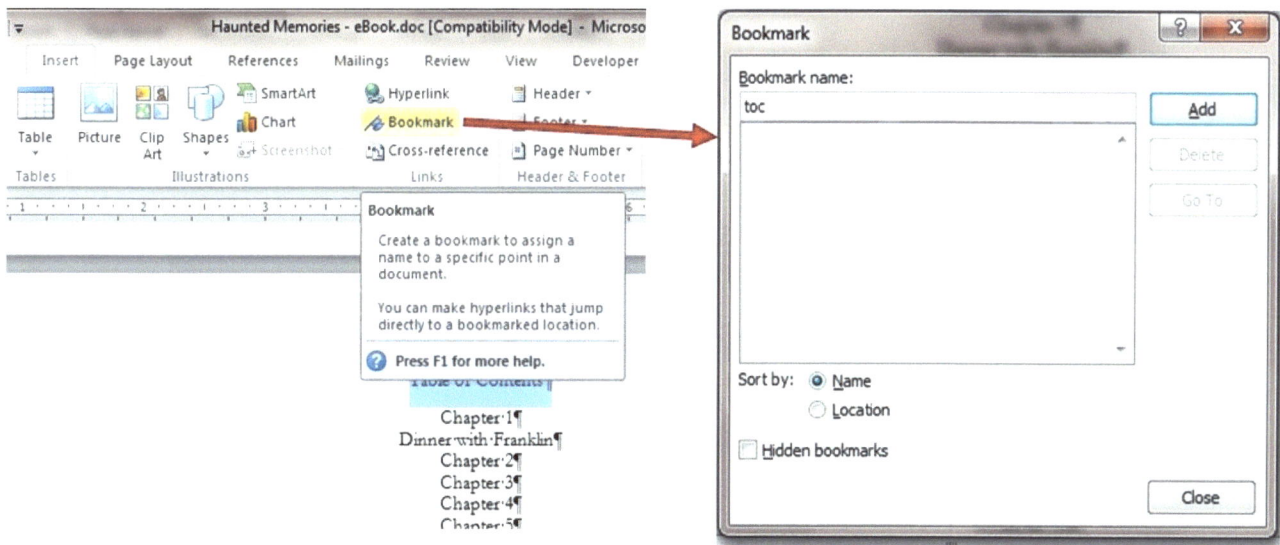

Figure 78. KDP—Bookmark Table of Contents (TOC)

Note: TOC is a standard Kindle bookmark, but not the others. To add a **List of Figures/Tables**, insert each similar to the TOC and bookmark the title as **lot/lof**. Then, type the title(s) into the TOC. Highlight this new text and <**Insert**> <**Hyperlink**> <**Place in this Document**> <**Bookmark**s> <**lof/lot**>.

6.6.4. Saving the File

The KDP documentation recommends saving the file as a filtered web page (.htm, .html). If there are images in your manuscript, they may not display properly as a web page. The .docx/.doc file can also be uploaded and it will handle the images. If you decide to use a filtered web page, perform the following steps. Navigate to <**File**> <**Save As**> and select <**Web Page, Filtered (*.htm, *.html)**> (**Figure 79**). When you click on <**Save**>, a warning box will appear (**Figure 80**). This reports that all Office specific tags will be removed. Since this is what you want, click on <**Yes**>. The file can now be uploaded to KDP.

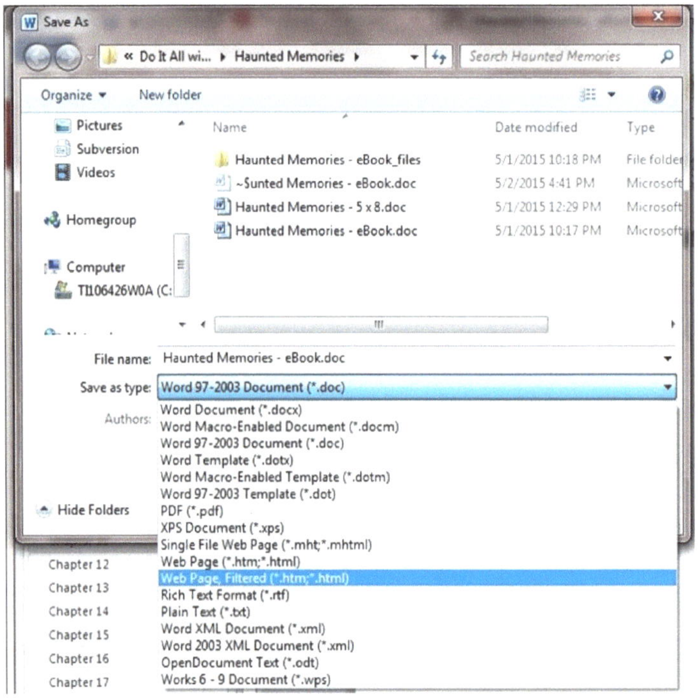

Figure 79. KDP—Saving the Word® Document as Filtered HTML

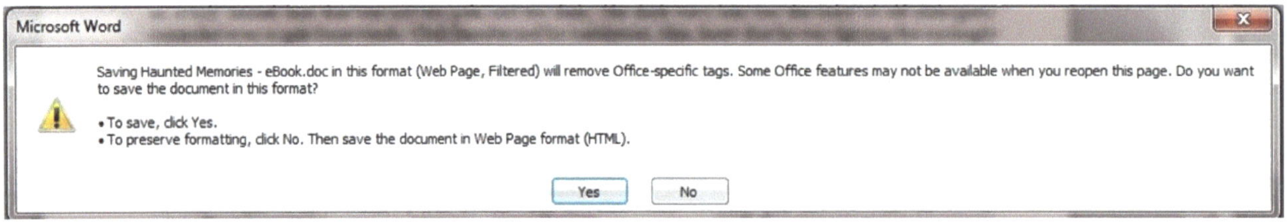

Figure 80. KDP—Saving the Word® Document as Filtered HTML - Warning

6.6.5. Uploading for Review

Once the file is ready for uploading, navigate to the KDP Project page for this book and scroll down to <**Upload Your Book File**>. Before uploading the file, select the <**Digital Rights Management (DRM)**> option, either <**Enable…**> or <**Do not enable…**> (**Figure 81**). If you enable DRM, the eBook can be shared, but only under Amazon control. If you do not enable DRM, anyone who obtains your book can share it with whomever they want, as many times as they want. Once you publish your book, the DRM cannot be changed. If you change the DRM option, you must save the project before continuing.

Click on <**Browse**> and upload the manuscript file.

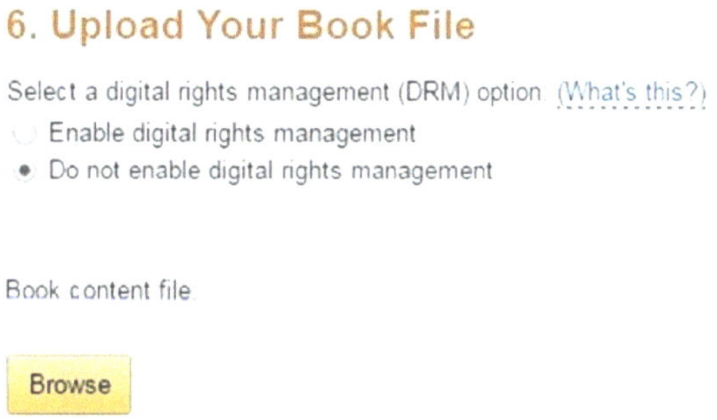
6. Upload Your Book File
Select a digital rights management (DRM) option (What's this?)
Enable digital rights management
Do not enable digital rights management
Book content file
Browse

Figure 81. KDP—Upload Your Book File – DRM Option

After a short time, the conversion will complete and you have the option to view the eBook with an <**Online Previewer**> and/or <**Download Book Preview File**> (**Figure 82**). The latter is a .mobi file, which can be viewed on a physical device. Once downloaded, connect your eBook device to your computer and copy the mobi file just as you would when transferring a file from/to a USB device.

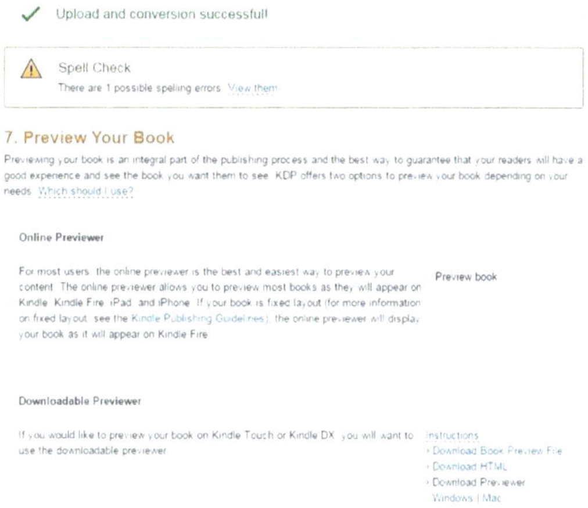
Upload and conversion successful!
Spell Check
7. Preview Your Book
Online Previewer
Preview book
Downloadable Previewer

Figure 82. KDP—Conversion Complete – Preview Options

At this point, if you're satisfied with your eBook, click on <**Save & Continue**>. If not, modify the original document, save as a filtered web page and upload it again. If you're unsure of formatting or how something will look, try it. You can always upload a new file if you're not happy with the results.

6.6.6. Distribution and Pricing

Publishing Territories (**Figure 83**): The hard work is all behind you – now it's time to determine where you'll distribute the book and how much you'll charge. You can choose one or all of 245 territories. I choose all. Why not?

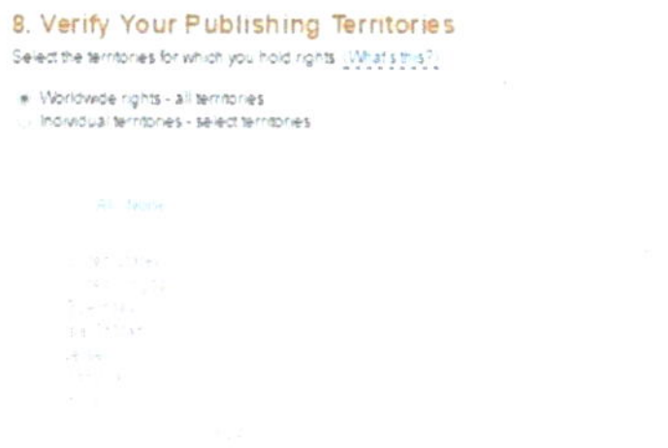
8. Verify Your Publishing Territories

Figure 83. KDP—Verify Publishing Territories

Pricing and Royalties (Figure 84): There are clickable links that detail how these options are handled. They're mostly in legal-ese, but should be read periodically. At the time of publication of this book, the 35% royalty applies if your book is below $2.99; 70% otherwise. You can select 35% for any price, but I'm not sure why you would. List price is whatever you believe the book is worth. A prevailing attitude is that since eBooks don't require an upfront investment, it's better to price them low and go for quantity. This is especially true if you're an unknown author.

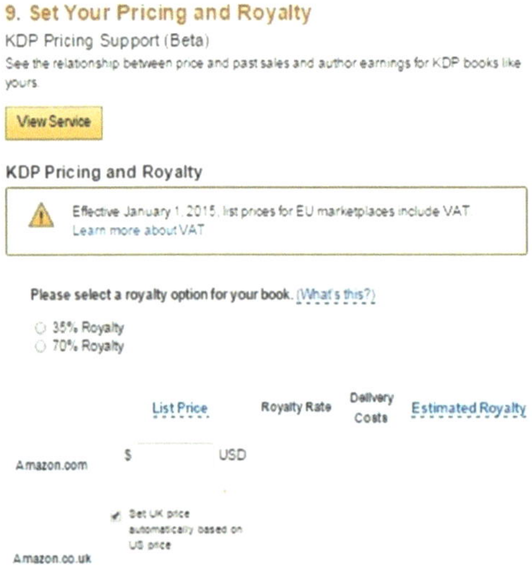

Figure 84. KDP—Pricing and Royalties

6.6.7. Kindle MatchBook and Book Lending

Scrolling past the pricing gets to the display shown in **Figure 85**. <**Kindle MatchBook**> refers to books that have an associated paperback. If you select <**MatchBook**>, if a customer buys the print version of the book, you can make the eBook available for free or for a reduced price, typically $0.99. I make the eBook available for free if the print version is purchased. <**Kindle Book Lending**> allows customers to loan the book to other users, one at a time.

Once these options have been considered and selected, click the <**Terms and Conditions**> check box to let KDP know you agree to their terms, then click on <**Save and Publish**>. After a short review time, typically 72 hours, your title will be ready for purchase on Amazon.

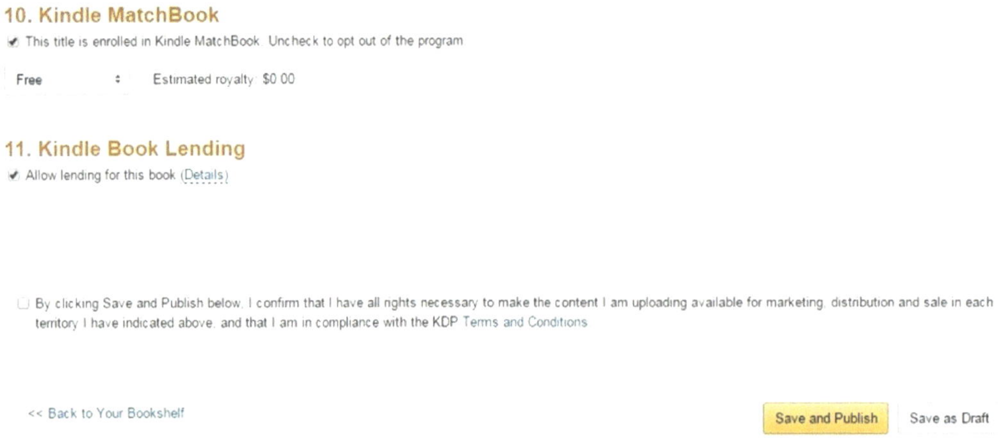

Figure 85. KDP—MatchBook, Lending and Publication

Chapter 7. **Published Author**

7.1. Live on Amazon / Author's Page

Once your book is live, whether paperback, eBook or both, navigate to https://authorcentral.Amazon.com and set up an author's page.   It's helpful to cut and paste the author's bio from your book page to maintain consistency and cut down on your work. Once this is complete, navigate to the <**Books**> tab and add your books. If you have a paperback/eBook pair, the two should automatically link as two different media of the same book.   If this doesn't happen within a reasonable amount of time (usually happens at time of publication), contact Amazon customer service.   The people are courteous, helpful and pretty much amazing. They'll assist in clearing up any issues with how your books are displayed.

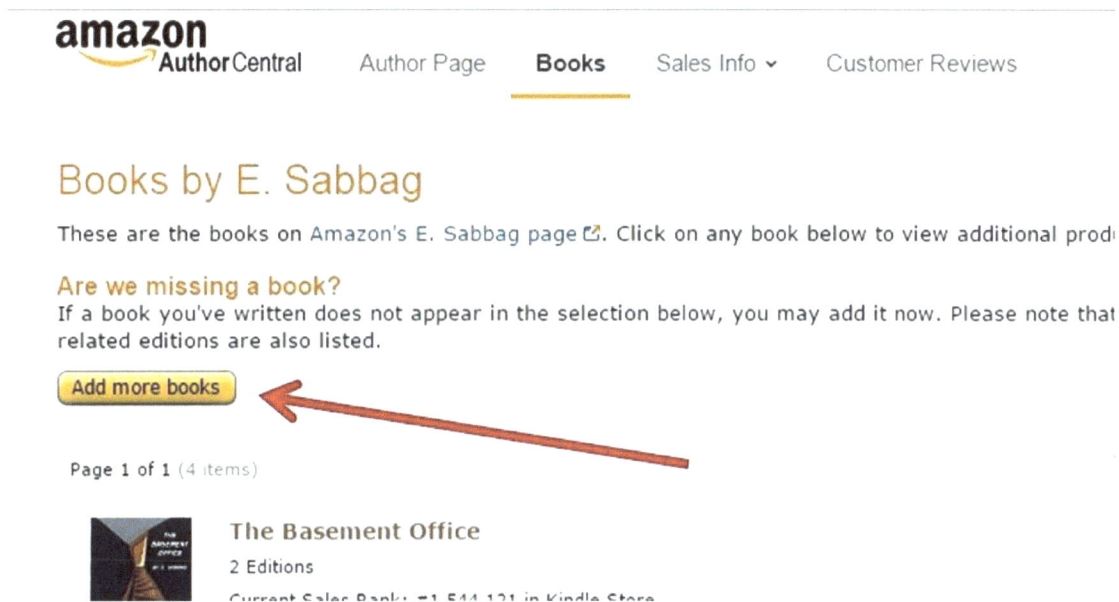

Figure 86. Author's Page - Adding Books

7.2. ISBN Setup

If you purchased ISBN's from Bowker, navigate to your account and update the information from both your POD and your eBook for each ISBN. Ensure the information syncs up with CS and KDP exactly.

7.3. Next Steps

Now that you have a POD paperback or an eBook or both, you are officially published. Time to celebrate! You've earned it. However, the book won't sell itself, no matter how good it is or how much your mother / father / siblings / children / friends / family love it. It takes work and dedication to start the next phase, which is marketing your work. Unfortunately, it's also beyond the scope of this book, but I wish you all the best. Good luck and let me know how you do.

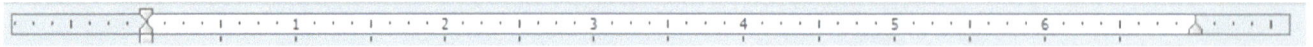

Chapter 8. **Setting up a CreateSpace Account**

This section is only required once, but I've included it because the tax information may be intimidating to a new author. Please note that I am a writer and an engineer, not a tax accountant. As such, this information is meant as a guideline. If you're uncomfortable with any of it, seek a professional. Regardless, be ethical / legal and pay any applicable taxes on your profits.

Navigate to the website www.CreateSpace.com. Click on **<Sign Up>** as indicated in **Figure 87. CS Website—Create New** Account.

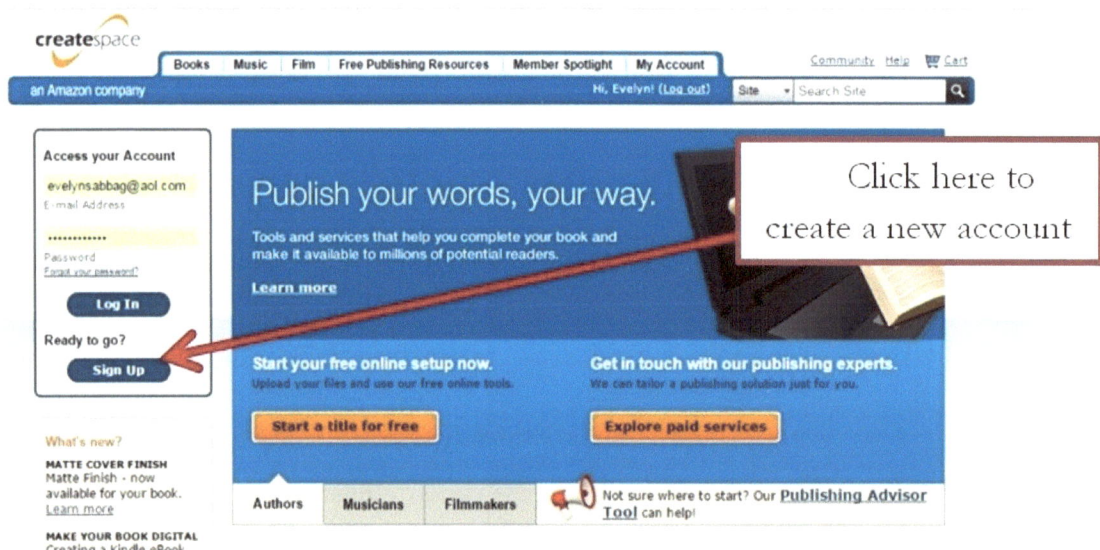

Figure 87. CS Website—Create New Account

Required information for a new account is minimal. Fill in the following fields as indicated in **Figure 88. CS Website—New Account Info:**

- Email
- Password (and confirmation)
- First Name
- Last Name
- Country
- Type of media (this can be changed later)
- Request for consultation (optional – leave blank)
- Update on promotions, newsletters, etc. (optional – leave blank)

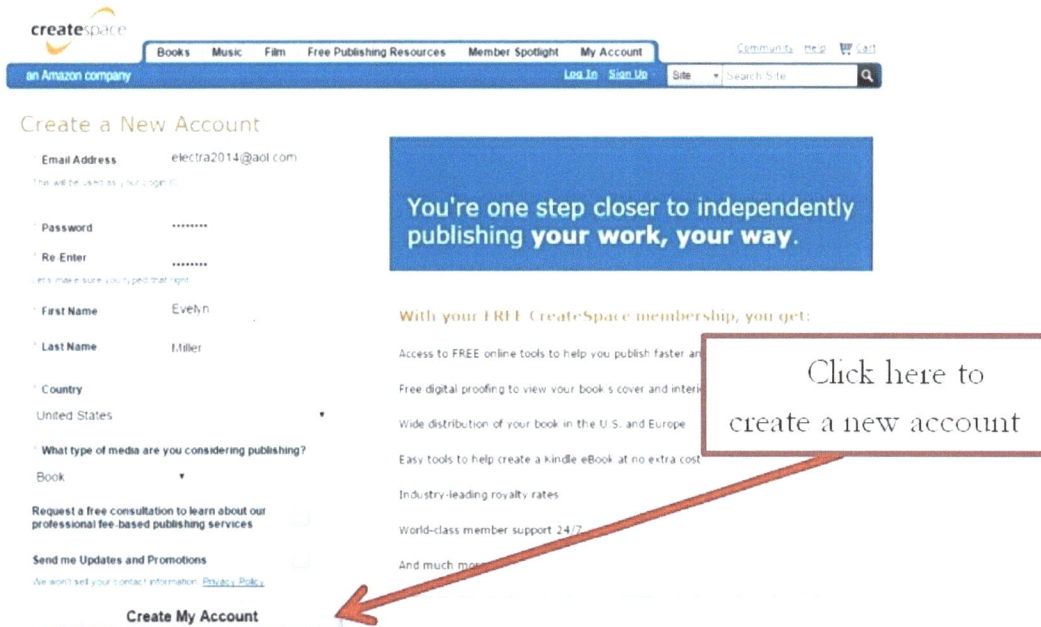

Figure 88. CS Website—New Account Info

Once you've filled in the information, click on **<Create My Account>**. This will bring up the screen indicated in **Figure 89**. After you've read through the Services Agreement, click on **<I agree to all…>**. If you don't agree, click on **<I do not agree to these terms>**. Unfortunately, if you don't agree, you can't continue. Sorry, but that's just the way it is. The rest of the sections on CS assume you've agreed to the Services Agreement.

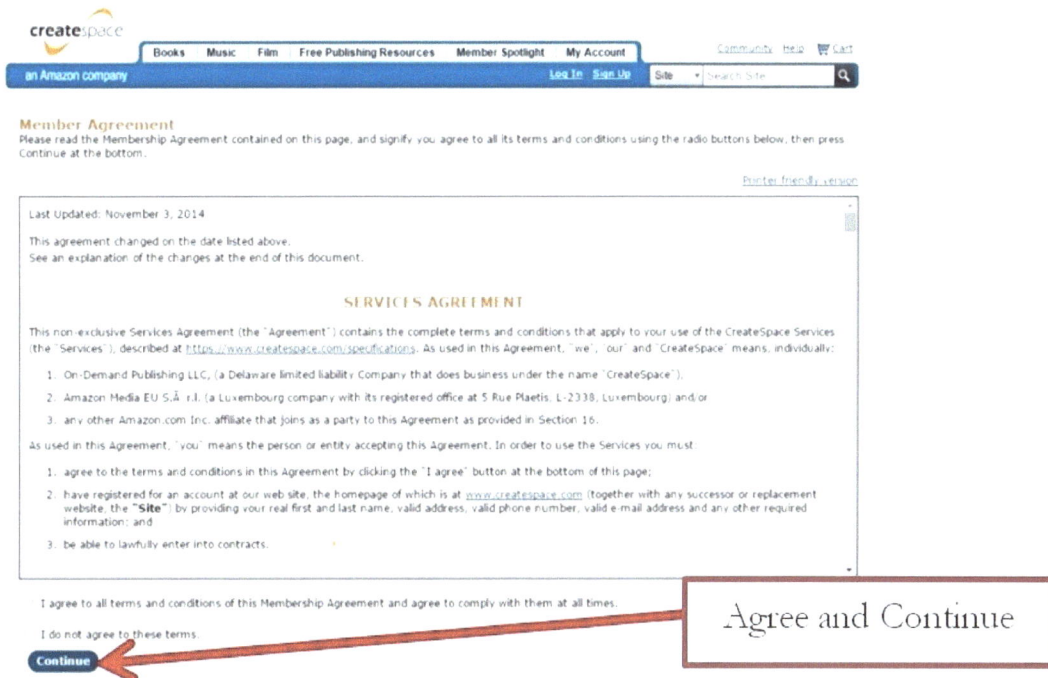

Figure 89. CS—Services Agreement

After you've clicked on **<Continue>**, the screen in **Figure 90** will appear.

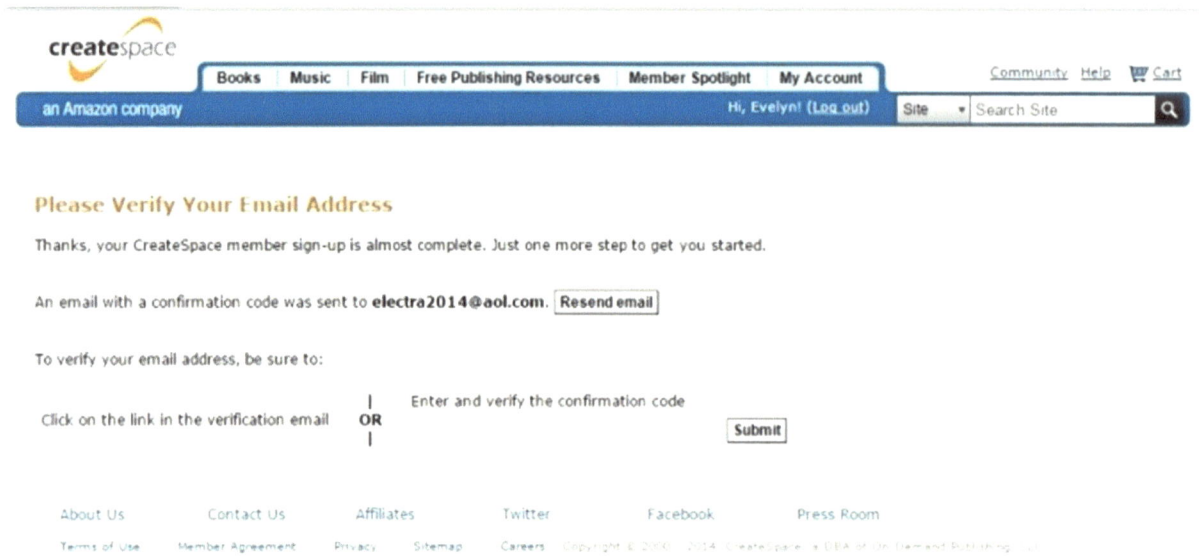

Figure 90. CS—Please Verify Your Email Address

Leave this screen active on your browser and monitor your email. When the verification email arrives (sample in **Figure 91**), follow the instructions.

Note: Each time I've set up a CreateSpace account, the email arrived within minutes. This is in contrast with other POD accounts, which have taken over a week to activate.

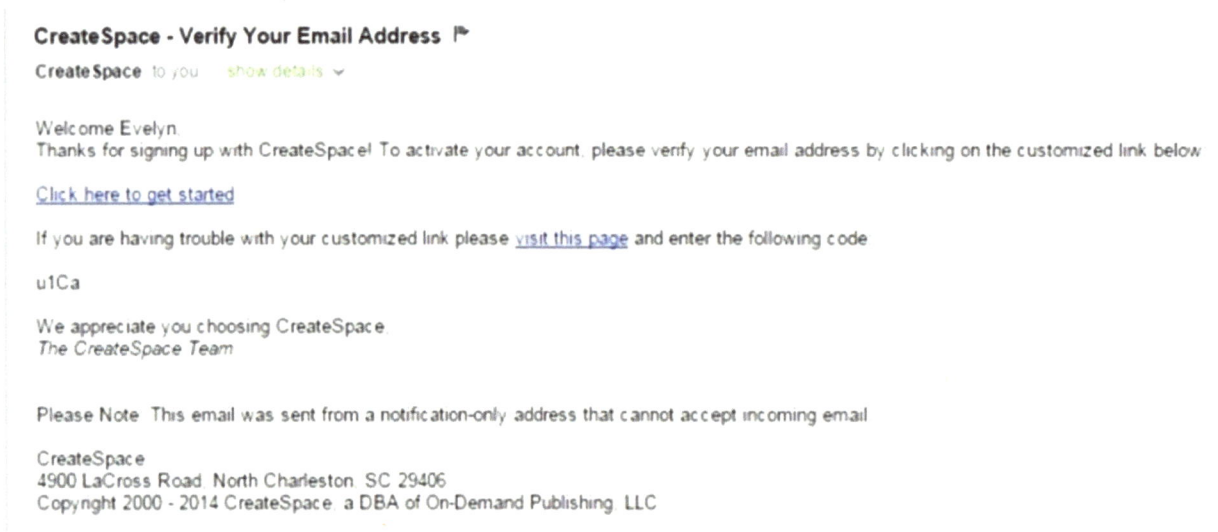

Figure 91. CS—Contents of Verification Email

Either click on the provided link <**Click here to get started**> or return to the active browser (**Figure 90**), fill in the confirmation code and click <**Submit**>.

Note: Your confirmation code will differ from that shown here.

The screen in **Figure 92** appears only once after account activation. There are better ways to set up projects, so for now, this can be ignored.

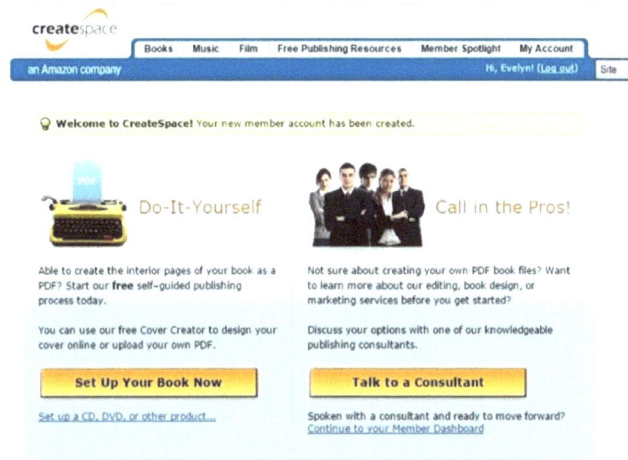

Figure 92. CS—New Project Welcome Screen

Congratulations! The account is set up and you're ready to build a book. Well, almost… What would a commercial enterprise be without taxes? In addition to the account activation email, the tax information request shown in **Figure 93** also arrives. Somewhat scary, but, like most CreateSpace requirements, easy enough.

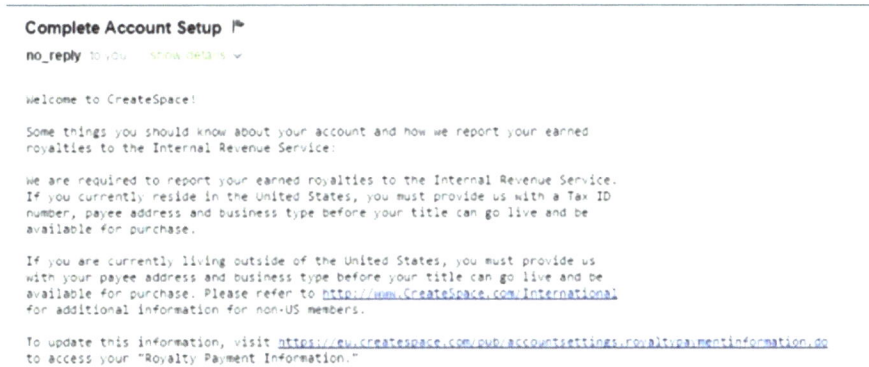

Figure 93. CS—Account Completion Email - Tax Information

Log out of your account and then log back in. The Welcome Screen (which never shows up again) disappears, replaced by the Member Dashboard. The tax information alert is at the top, as indicated by **Figure 94**.

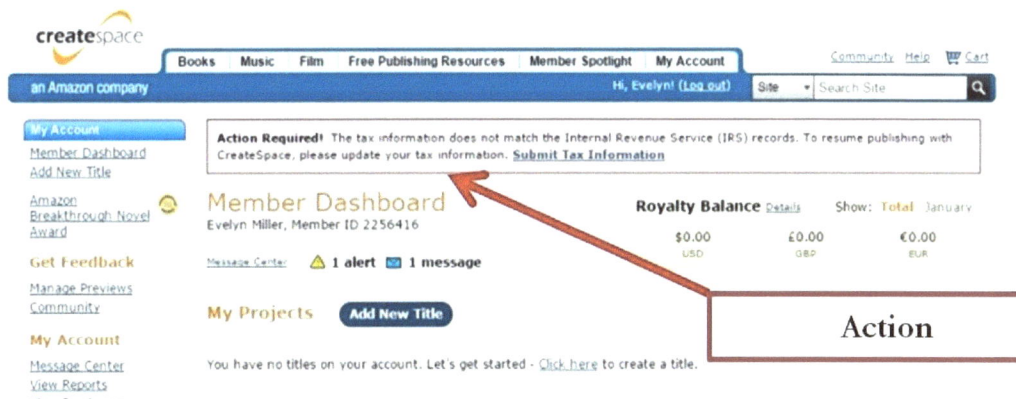

Figure 94. CS—Member Dashboard - Tax Information Alert

Click on <**Message Center**> and the display in **Figure 95** will appear.

Evelyn Sabbag

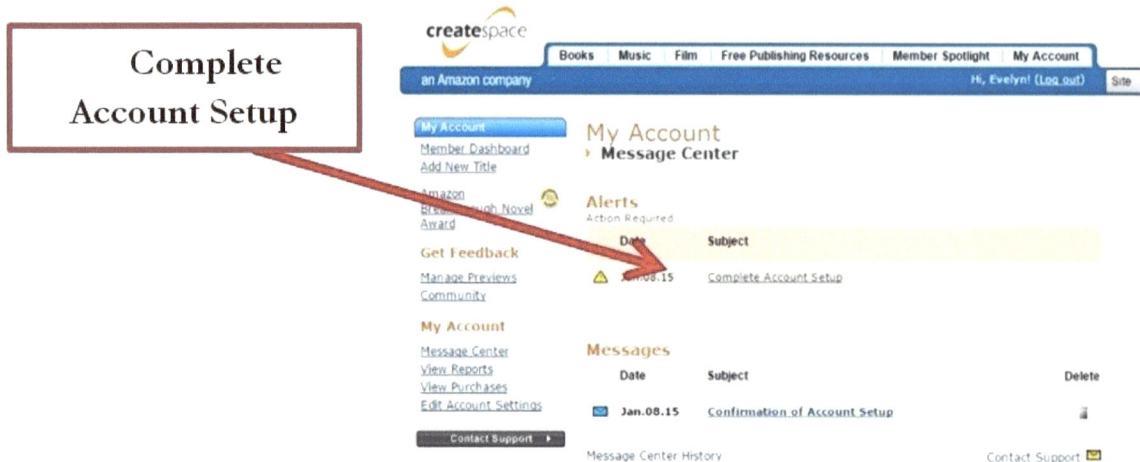

Figure 95. CS—Message Center - Account Activation Messages

Click on the alert <**Complete Account Setup**> to access the message. At the bottom of the message, click on <**Start fixing this issue**> (**Figure 96**).

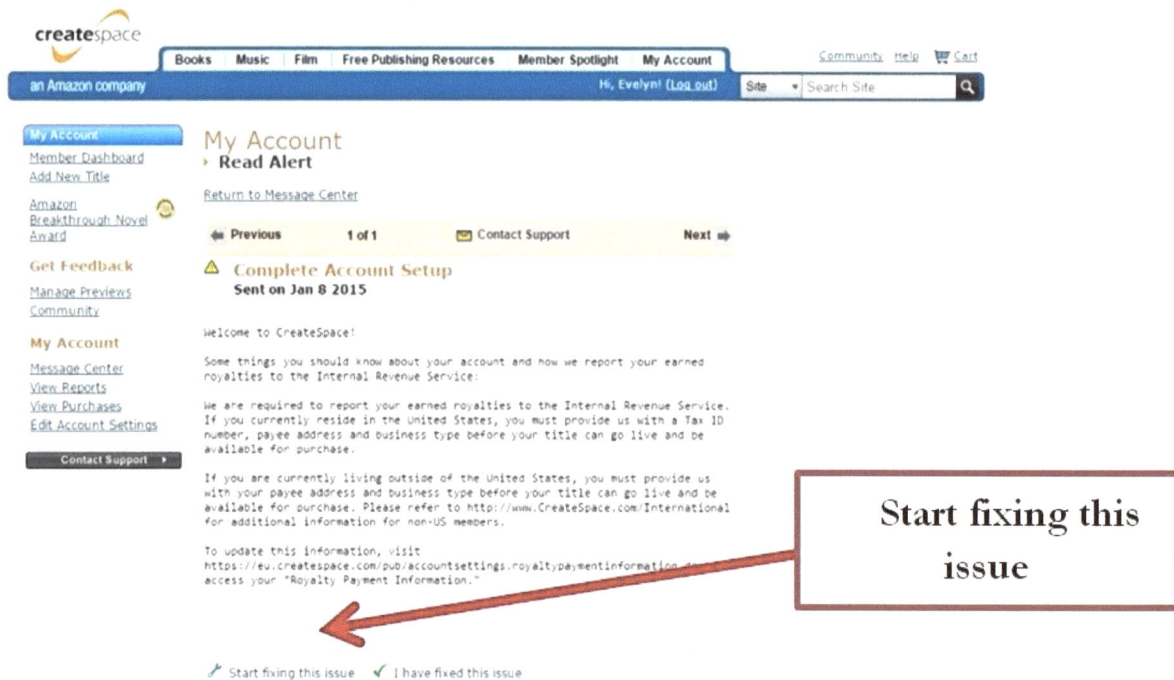

Figure 96. CS—Message Center Alert - Complete Account Setup

The great news about the next screen is that CreateSpace assumes you'll make money on your book! Fill in the appropriate information (payment type can be changed at any future time) and click on <**Submit Tax Information**> (**Figure 97**).

Note: If you select <**Check**>, a $8/€8/£8 fee is assessed each time a check is issued and will not be triggered until $100/€100/£100 worth of royalties are accumulated. This is a total of $108/€108/£108 worth of books must be sold before you receive anything. Direct deposit is paid quarterly, regardless of amount. My preference is <**Direct Deposit**>, but you will have to supply your bank account number and routing number. After working with CreateSpace for over six years, I've never had a problem with anyone hacking my bank account or other financial irregularities.

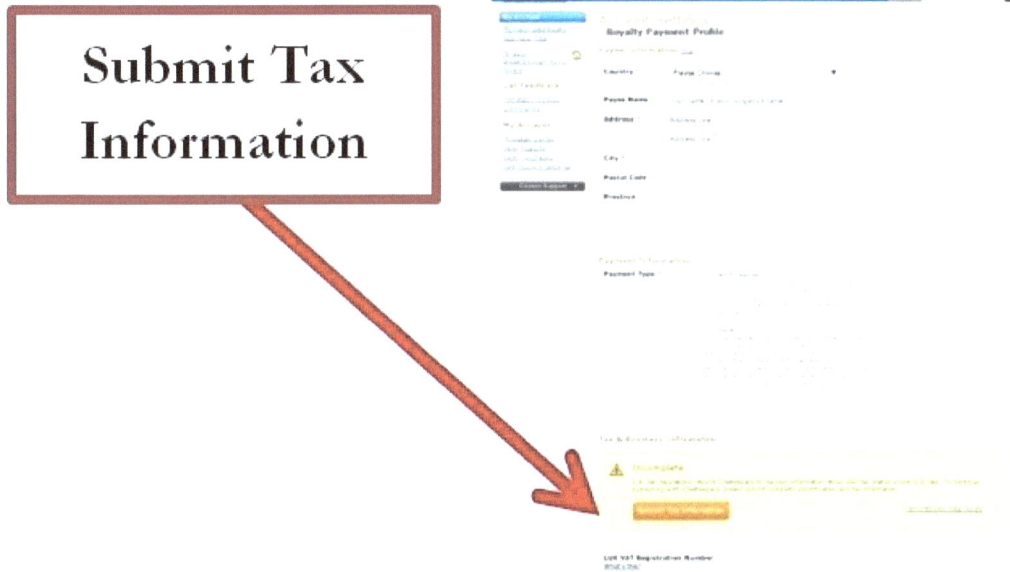

Figure 97. CS—Royalty Payment Profile

A Tax Information Interview follows. Fill in the information as directed, clicking on <**Save and Continue**> after each section. At the end, click on <**Exit Interview**>. This should result in the screen in **Figure 98**. Any issues are beyond the scope of this book. *I'm an author, not a tax accountant, Jim.*

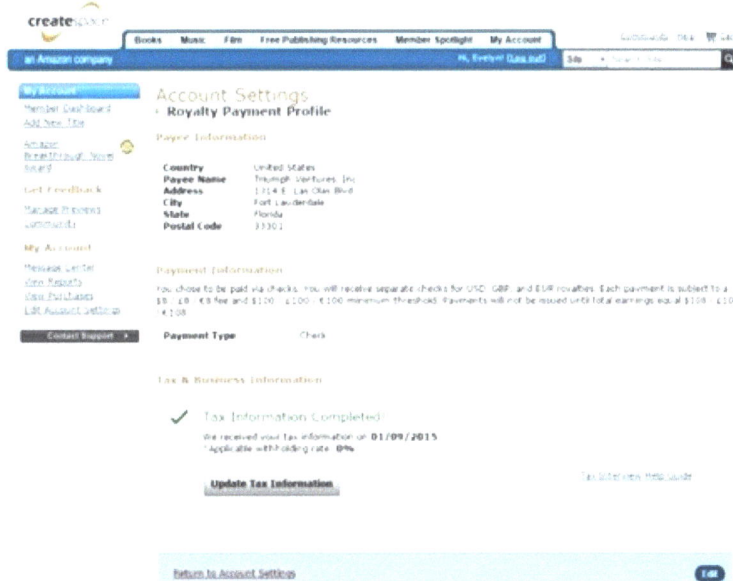

Figure 98. CS—Royalty Payment Profile Completed

Now you can return to the Member Dashboard, then Message Center, open the Alert and click on <**I have fixed this issue**> (**Figure 96**). This will remove the alert from the Message Center and the Member Dashboard. At this time, you can also read the message that comes along with the Account Activation.

About the Author

Evelyn Sabbag is a sailor, educator, engineer, and, primarily, a writer. She has self-published several non-fiction and fiction works. One novel, *Workshop 'Til You Drop*, was a Quarter Finalist in the 2014 Amazon Breakthrough Novel Award. While working in the technology industry, she achieved her Microsoft Office User Specialist (MOUS) Certification as well as wrote numerous users' and instructional manuals. A US Coast Guard Certified captain, she's a fulltime live-aboard and cruises the world with her husband aboard their ketch-rigged sailboat.

All novels, fiction and non-fiction can be found through her website, www.TriumphCharters.com/books.html. She writes in several genres, including traditional murder mysteries, paranormal romance, psychological horror and memoirs based on her adventures on and off shore.

www.ingramcontent.com/pod-product-compliance
Lightning Source LLC
Chambersburg PA
CBHW041425090426
42741CB00002B/39